PSALM TWENTY-THREE
AN ANTHOLOGY

Psalm Twenty-Three

AN ANTHOLOGY

Versions Collected
and Annotated by
K. H. STRANGE
and
R. G. E. SANDBACH

THE SAINT ANDREW PRESS
EDINBURGH

Originally published as *Psalm 23: Several Versions Collected and Put Together* by K. H. Strange 1969

Republished 1970 by The Saint Andrew Press

Revised and extended edition published 1978 by
THE SAINT ANDREW PRESS
121 George Street, Edinburgh

ISBN 0 7152 0374 6

Printed and bound in Great Britain by
Morrison & Gibb Ltd, London and Edinburgh

Contents

The songs are these, which Heaven's high Holy Muse
Whisper'd to David, David to the Jewes:
And David's successors, in holy zeale
In formes of joy and art doe re-reveale.

Dr John Donne, Dean of St Paul's (1572–1631) in 'The Translation of the Psalmes by Sir Philip Sidney, and the Countesse of Pembroke his sister'

Foreword to 1969 Anthology

I have been looking at the Top Ten for last week, and wondering how long these best-selling songs will last. Which will still be sung in a twelve-month's time?

A glance at Kathleen Strange's Contents list is a reminder that this song, which we know as the Twenty-third Psalm, has already been going for perhaps two and a half thousand years. We cannot date the Hebrew version precisely. Many of the Psalms belong to the tragic period of their history when the Jews were exiled in Babylon: others are no doubt much earlier.

But this lack of accurate dating does not matter, for the Psalms are poetry and sing of timeless themes. Men and women of every generation, and of every language into which they have been rendered, have found their experience responding to these themes, and have taken the Psalms to their hearts. The early Christians went to martyrdom with 'The Lord is my shepherd' on their lips: Augustine loved it: George Herbert paraphrased it: Ruskin learned to say it for his mother. In our own day it is sung at the wedding of Queen and commoner.

And it will go on like that, because life will not basically alter, however much the trappings change. We shall always feel the need for company, especially in the dark and in the storm. The Bible is above all a book about what men like ourselves have found in God; and in the Twenty-third Psalm one of these men, whose name we do not even know, set down for us how he got on in the valley of the shadow as well as by green pastures; how he kept his hope alive and found that at journey's end it was a coming home.

Some of the versions in this collection are fun. The point is that the 'shepherd' theme can be transposed into other keys for those who know nothing about sheep but all about support and care and guidance, and the original message comes through just the same.

Kathleen Strange means her Anthology to be used for sheer enjoyment. As each reader joins her he too may feel like C. S. Lewis who said about his reading of the Psalms: 'I walk in wonders beyond myself'.

July 1969   E. C. D. STANFORD

Preface

The book which I published in 1969: *Psalm 23: Several Versions* contained a very short foreword and twenty-six versions of the psalm, to most of which I added a brief explanatory footnote. All that I wanted to do was to present some of the more significant of the fifty or more versions of Psalm 23 that had come my way, and to let them speak for themselves.

In the intervening period I have acquired more versions, many of them from people who possessed a copy of my book and who wished to pass on to me something extra which the book lacked: another translation, a commentary, a meditation in verse or prose.

In sorting out this material, I have found myself wanting to produce a book which would appeal to my readers, and there must be some thousands of them, for the book has been reprinted several times.

I find I have now well over a hundred versions; I showed them to R. G. E. Sandbach and we discussed what should be done with them, and our discussions have eventually led to this book.

Our attention has been drawn to two other versions of Psalm 23, but unfortunately too late to be seen before going to press. These are of some historical importance and are in the Psalters translated by Matthew Parker (1505–1575), Elizabeth I's first Archbishop of Canterbury, and George Sandys (1578–1644), traveller and poet, published respectively in 1567 and 1636. It should also be noted that a new translation of the Psalms, the work of four Fellows of St John's College, Cambridge, was published in 1977. This unfortunately cannot be included either. It is felt, however, that mention should be made of these translations.

K. H. Strange

PART I

INTRODUCTION

1. Some General Remarks

The versions fall into groups and this new edition contains a selection of eighty-seven from the hundred and more versions; all the versions contained in the 1969 book are reprinted here.

We have had in mind several objectives—to avoid monotony, to emphasise the universality and topicality of the psalm, and to give examples illustrating the variety of human needs, some of them mentioned by those who contributed the versions. Above all we wanted to encourage every reader to say with C. S. Lewis: 'I walk in wonders beyond myself.'

The book is not intended to be read at a sitting—though if any reader does go from the first page to the last, we should like to think of him with pencil in hand, marking the versions which have special relevance for him. It is interesting to learn that the prolific Wesleys who were stirring up the people, educated and not educated, into religious enthusiasm wrote a number of metrical versions, before hymn-singing was an accepted practice in churches; that the Victorians produced version after version expressing Victorianism in their search for truth; that twenty or more Scottish versions, some of them needing a Gaelic–English Dictionary, reached us from Scotland, Canada and elsewhere; that in our own day young people have produced their own contemporary versions, to prove to themselves, and to the older generation, the continuing relevance of the psalm.

In addition to all this, the scholars of our own time—of this second half of the twentieth century—have produced their own versions, going back to the original Hebrew, studying St Jerome's version, reading the early Anglo-Saxon versions, and endeavouring to retain the style and rhythm of the best version of them all—that of 1611.

3

We have read, and been deeply impressed by *The Psalms in Human Life* (1903) by E. R. Prothero (1862–1937) who became Lord Ernle. In this book, the author shows the influence of the Psalms on religious people from the earliest times until the nineteenth century. Prothero had the advantage of discussing the idea of the book with and using the notes of A. P. Stanley, the famous Dean of Westminster and an ecclesiastical historian of note in Victorian times. There is no doubt that the most impressive part of the book is the first half, covering ancient mediaeval and Reformation times, when men inflicted torture and death in its most horrible forms on their fellow-men in the name of religion, with a cruelty only equalled by certain twentieth-century dictators like Stalin and Hitler. But what is most striking is that the singing of certain psalms at a moment of crisis and horror appeared to have an almost miraculous and ecstatic effect on the sufferers in times of danger and distress. What effect this had on those present we can only guess at, but someone was sufficiently moved to record the martyrs' utterances. Then it must be remembered that the Dark Age hermits were in the habit of chanting the whole of the Psalms in three stages.

Prothero tells us that St Augustine of Hippo especially chose the 23rd Psalm as the Hymn of the Martyrs and the number of them was tragically great in those days.

Today there can be little doubt that the 23rd Psalm is the universal favourite. Someone should write an up-to-date book on the lines of Prothero's historical one, for there are many stories in modern times of the effect that this Psalm has had on people in a crisis. Since the publication of *Psalm 23 : Several Versions* in 1969, we have learned from correspondence, or from the media, or in conversation with people, of such things as the following:

An Australian Methodist, meeting members of her Church on her travels in New Guinea, sent us the pidgin English version. Captain Booker—an old man in 1969—wrote from Vancouver to confirm that he still remembered singing the Pilot's Version of the Psalm at a funeral service on board ship in 1906. A clergyman wrote of his uncle, the mountaineer, who composed the Mountaineer's Psalm. A visitor to a dying patient in St Barnabas' Home, Worthing, found the patient in tranquil mood: 'I was

4

feeling a bit low,' the young dying patient said, 'and then the American-Indian Psalm 23 came over the loudspeaker and I felt all right.' School chaplains have entered into correspondence; a choirmaster in Canada sent his own composition for accompanying the Japanese version and said he composed it to be 'singable and enjoyable'. A headmistress said she was constantly re-reading this Japanese version because it reduced the stress caused by her job. A nonagenarian wrote asking for a copy to send to an old friend—a duchess wrote saying she kept running out of copies for her friends—a man dossing in a shelter asked for a copy. A reader sent in an ironical paraphrase, satirising trade unionism. An old Sussex antiquarian recorded two Sussex versions in authentic Sussex dialect and these were broadcast on Radio Brighton. We have folders full of interesting letters, sent in by readers of the 1969 book.

We have been frequently reminded of the many attempts made by people to get rid of stumbling-blocks in the understanding of the Bible by the man in the street. The very title of a book by the late Baroness Stocks, *Unread Best-Seller*, is significant of what she tried to do: to pass on her own excitement of discovering the relevance of the Old Testament to contemporary life.

Baroness Stocks was only doing what progressive and thoughtful people have done throughout the centuries: interpreted the Bible in their own modern idiom, so that it should not be thought of as a secret, chained-up book for intellectuals and holy people, but as a book that is understandable by all.

The aim of the Introduction to this anthology is to show quite briefly the influence of David and the 23rd Psalm on humanity from his day to ours. We have mentioned by name certain translators and scholars and other writers who would disclaim the name of scholar. It must be emphasised that all of these are not of equal value from one viewpoint or another, and they are not to be judged from the amount of space allocated to them. 'There were giants in the earth in those days' and there were giants among the early translators, and contemporary translators pay tribute to them. It was found by the Committee of 1604–1611 that

5

Tyndale and Coverdale could often not be improved upon by them. These two, together with St Jerome and John Wycliffe, were among the world's greatest Biblical Scholars, translators and not mere paraphrasers, men who were dedicated to the service of God and gave their talents to humanity. St Paul reminds us of them when he is explaining that there are varieties of gifts but the same spirit: 'One man, through the Spirit, has the gift of wise speech, while another, by the power of the same spirit, can put the deepest knowledge into words . . .'

The twentieth-century scholars who produced the New English Bible in 1970 must have thought of the giant translators of the past when working at their modern translation, and they paid tribute to them and the members of the 1611 Committee which produced the beloved Authorised Version of the Bible.

2. *Authorship of the Psalms in general and the Development of the Psalter*

There is no one who would deny that 'The Psalms of David' is one of the most important books in Hebrew, and, later, in Christian worship, but that it is also one of the masterpieces of world literature.

It is an anthology of religious verse intended to be sung at devotions and its original name means 'praises'.

But how right are we in calling the work 'The Psalms of David'? This now is a very difficult question to answer and one on which there is disagreement among Biblical scholars. Rightly or wrongly, practically all the psalms have been ascribed to various authors, some of them highly distinguished. For instance, the first of the five books is thought by many scholars to be almost entirely the work of King David, to whom, in fact, seventy-three of the one hundred and fifty psalms have been ascribed. Solomon, Moses, Jeremiah, Hezekiah, and Haggai have been named as authors of others, besides certain Temple musicians of whom we know little, such as Asaph, Heman, Ethan, Jedtham, and the Sons of Korah. Other psalms clearly belong to the period of the Babylonian Captivity, in the seventh and eighth centuries BC.

In his book *David* (1943), Duff Cooper writes thus on this problem of King David's share in writing the Psalms:

'The question of their authorship is a problem for scholars who cannot hope to find a final solution. It is certain they cannot all have been written by David because some of them refer explicitly to events which occurred many centuries after his death. Here again, however, there is a tendency for doubt to go to extremes, and the fact that David did not write all the Psalms has led some critics to the conclusion that he wrote none of them. . . . It must be remembered that what appears incredible to scholars of the nineteenth and twentieth centuries was accepted without difficulty by scholars who were two thousand years nearer to David than we are. . . .'

But how long it took the Psalms to be edited into their present form, is another and more difficult question. It would be considerably after the Captivity but probably not as late as the time of the Maccabees (167 BC to 37 BC) as some scholars in the early part of the twentieth century claimed.

3. *Hymns versus Psalms in England*
In England, with the coming of printing (and even before) the Psalms became the chief mode of musical expression in Church services, until the great hymns of the early eighteenth century replaced them to some extent (and only to some extent). This, rather curiously, seems to have been due to Nonconformist influence. As the Methodist Hymn Book stated: 'Methodism was born in song'.

Although hymns had been written and sung by Christian communities, along with the Psalms, from the time of the early Christian Fathers, it was Isaac Watts (1674–1748), an Independent Minister, who wrote the first really great English hymns. He also wrote a complete metrical Psalter, some psalms being in various versions. Then, in 1739, came Methodism. All the Wesleys were accomplished musicians and Charles Wesley (1707–1788) was an inspired, if unequal, poet with some great hymns to his credit among a lot that were indifferent.

It was these men who started the great hymn revival which relegated the psalm to the less important place it now holds in the religious services of this country.

The first really popular complete Psalter was that of

7

Thomas Sternhold (1500–1549), Groom of Robes to Henry VIII, and the Reverend John Hopkins; this was published in 1562, thirteen years after Sternhold's death. This metrical version held its place in the affections of the people until the publication of the complete metrical translation of Nahum Tate (1652–1715) and Nicolas Brady (1659–1726) of 1696. The Metrical Psalter of Isaac Watts of 1718 was hardly less popular. Nevertheless, none of these translations has much literary merit.

Nowadays, the version of the Psalms most commonly used is that of the 'Common Prayer Book', mainly by Miles Coverdale, but much influenced by William Tyndale. It is echoed in the Authorised Version of the Bible and is perhaps nearly its equal in literary merit. Dr Richard Garnett, speaking of the greater popular appeal of Sternhold and Hopkins' metrical version, wrote of the latter:

'It is a work of necessity rather than mercy and it is surprising that its imperfections should have been so meekly tolerated by an age which possessed the noble translations of the Prayer Book and Bible.'

Another critic, Dr E. A. Baker, wrote:

'Coverdale's memorial, is, of course, the Psalter in the English Prayer Book which is unsurpassed in its rhythmical beauty.'

Yet perhaps we can understand the greater popularity of Sternhold and Hopkins. On the title page of early editions of this work is printed, after the title, the following:

'Newly set out and allowed to be sung in all Churches, of all people together, before and after the sermons. Moreover, in private houses, for their goodly solace and comfort; laying apart all ungodly songs and ballads which may tend onely to the nourishing of vice and corrupting of youth.'

In other words, Sternhold and Hopkins was a good, safe, family sing-song book.

In the *Journal* of George Fox, the founder of the Society of Friends, we read under 1642:

'After that I went to another ancient priest in Mancetter, in Warwickshire, and reasoned with him about the grounds of despair and temptation; but he bade me to take tobacco and sing Psalms. Tobacco was a thing I did not love and Psalms, I was not in a state to sing; I could not sing.'

I am sure that ancient priest sang Sternhold and Hopkins. It is interesting that he considered tobacco and psalm-singing a good cure for depression. One feels that the mixture would be convivial. And why should there not be some conviviality?

4. The Scope of this Collection

Obviously every translation of the 23rd Psalm known to the compilers could not be included. It has, for example, been considered superfluous to include two versions by the same translator—even in the case of Isaac Watts who did several interesting renderings.

But besides being a mere collection of versions of one much-loved poem (which in itself is reason enough), it is hoped that it will give some idea of the often dramatic story of the diffusion of the Bible. We start with the original Psalm, the importance of early Hebrew Literature having been stressed by Duff Cooper in the dedication of his book *David*. It runs thus:

'To the Jewish People
to whom the world owes
the Old and New Testaments
and much else
in the realms of beauty and knowledge,
a debt that has been ill repaid.'

We then proceed to St Jerome who lived on the verge of 'the Dark Ages' and witnessed the appalling disaster of the fall of Rome. Thence, we proceed through the time of Wycliffe to the Reformation and the Counter-Reformation, a period when translating the Bible could incur the death penalty, as indeed it did in the case of William Tyndale. It was a period when translation could be used as a religious weapon. Many of the translators of sixteenth-century versions were refugees from the pro-Catholic persecutions under Queen Mary and (if not in this Psalm) their sectarianism often shows. The 'Geneva Bible' for example, is

9

strongly Calvinistic. Then we come to the major translation of Psalm 23, that of the Authorised Version of 1611. Thence, we travel through the dignified versions of the 'Augustan Age', (1660–1750) so called because its correctness of form recalled the Age of the Emperor Augustus when Horace, Virgil and Ovid lived. After that, we come to the stately versions of the Victorians until we reach the more colloquial and varied renderings of our own time.

A few translations and paraphrases have been omitted which possibly some would have liked included. There is, for instance, a version by Mary Baker Eddy, founder of Christian Science. It appears in her book: *Science and Health* (1875) but this, by virtue of certain alterations in the text of the Authorised Version, is more in the nature of an explanation: she would have described it as a 'Key' to the Psalm.

Equally interesting, although perhaps not relevant to this collection, are the meditations on the 23rd Psalm by Patience Strong who brings it to a more popular audience than it has usually, in the past, enjoyed. Typical of the effort to apply the Psalm to the needs of selected individuals is a pamphlet of *Pastoral Meditations* on the Psalm, composed by an American Hospital Chaplain and given to patients on admission to hospital; it was intended to give patients a further interpretation which they could apply to their own circumstances.

Many have heard of David Scott Blackhall, announcer for some years of the weekly 'In Touch' programmes on the BBC. Perhaps not everyone knows that he is a poet and that he wrote a sonnet sequence as a meditation on the 23rd Psalm. But it was more than a meditation; it was a therapy as he called it, for in middle age he had gone blind.

The Song of our Syrian Guest by William Allen Knight went through numerous editions in the early part of this century; our copy belonged to the edition of 505th thousand. The writer, who had indeed met a Syrian guest, wrote the book 'in a time of pain and shock' and found that he could bear the shock and pain by meditating on each sentence of Psalm 23. The meditations of Leslie Farmer on the 23rd Psalm in *I Lack Nothing* (1967) are also valuable and significant. So also are the thoughts of Phillip Keller in *A*

Shepherd Looks at Psalm 23 (1970). He calls himself 'a down-to-earth, hard-handed sheep man'; he has been not only a sheep rancher but also the lay pastor of a human 'flock' in a community church.

The purposes of translating, paraphrasing and meditating on the 23rd Psalm are endless.

5. The Music of the Psalms

The Psalms were, of course, written to be accompanied by vocal and instrumental music. We know very little about this music apart from the fact that it was probably influenced by that of the countries around Israel, especially Egypt. To the modern ear, it would probably appear harsh and cacophonous.

There were short simple melodies and no harmony. We know what the instruments were. The stringed instruments were the harp and the psaltery, the wind instrument was a kind of flute, possibly with a reed, while the percussion instruments were the tabrets, rather like cymbals, and another pair of wood instruments similar to castanets. The whole body of instruments joined in for the grand bursts of the chorus.

As Sir John Stainer (1840–1901), not only a great authority on ancient music, but a musician himself, wrote: 'But simple instruments such as harps, trumpets and cymbals when used in large numbers simultaneously or in alternating masses are capable of grand musical results.'

The congregation did not join the singing except for the 'Amen'. The singers and instrumentalists were Temple professionals and some of them at least were composers. The names of some of them are known and have already been mentioned but Asaph was probably the most famous in his time, apart from David himself.

The antiphonal treatment of the Psalms—that is to say, alternating passages being sung by different sections of the choir—goes back at least to the Temple of Solomon's time, according to the general belief.

Later the tendency of the recitation to develop into a monotone resulted in plainsong.

The oldest of the settings now commonly used is the Gregorian chant of the Roman Catholic Church. It is

11

named after St Gregory the Great, Pope from AD 590 to 640, who appears to have been responsible for its introduction. It is antiphonal, but in this case sung by Priest and Choir. The more recent but still time-honoured setting of the English Church, the Anglican Chant, is again antiphonal but usually sung by two sides of the choir. Other famous musical settings are 'The Seven Penitential Psalms' by Orlandus Lassus (1565) and 'The First Fifty Psalms' by Marcello (1724–1727).

There are also Psalm Settings by such famous composers as Bach, Mendelssohn and Franck, etc.

Dame Clara Butt (1873–1936) recorded the 23rd Psalm (from 'Four Biblical Songs' i.e. 23rd, 97th, 55th and 119th Psalms by Dvorak) in 1927 at Christchurch, Westminster Bridge Road, accompanied by band, piano and organ.

6. David in the Arts

It is not surprising that a character so versatile and universal as David should attract the attention of creative artists of all sorts who represent him in his various aspects. But it is usually the youthful David whom they interpret.

We see him in a Gothic illuminated manuscript of the thirteenth century as a peasant shepherd surrounded by sheep and goats, his pipes in his hand and his crook and harp on the ground beside him. Not an impressive David, this, but a homely figure who would appeal to the simple man.

We see him in copperplate engravings in eighteenth-century Psalters as the venerable musician—king and poet, crowned, bearded and dignified. But it is the sculptured Davids from Italy which are the most famous and these are all of the young David who slew Goliath.

First in time is the bronze statue by Donatello which belongs to about 1430. The young boy, rather feminine in appearance, is holding the giant's sword and gazing down at the helmeted head which he has just stricken from the giant's body. David is nude but for the greaves upon his legs and a curious helmet of no particular period on his head. A surprised smile flickers over his face.

Next we have the great marble statue of Michelangelo (1502) of a graceful, nude David lightly balanced on his legs, his sling ready to be discharged. It is classical in style and one of the masterpieces of the High Renaissance.

12

A more savage David, also in marble, is that of Lorenzo Bernini (1623) in the Galleria Borghese. This is no beautiful youth but a hard-faced peasant boy with rough skins round his waist. The statue is full of action. He is in the act of discharging the stone from his sling and his mouth is pursed and grim. It has none of the softness of the earlier statues.

In painting, the story of David has also been treated in oils in three thoroughly pre-Raphaelite pictures by D. G. Rossetti in Llandaff Cathedral; they were painted between 1860 and 1864. The first is 'David as Shepherd' and shows him going forth to fight Goliath with crook and sling, while just behind, faintly visible, is the massed army of Israel. The second is 'David as King'. He is seated, crowned, playing upon his harp and is, rather curiously, clad in chain mail of the twelfth century AD. A third in the series called 'The Seed of David' shows the infant Jesus with his mother.

In churches throughout the country there are representations of David in stained-glass windows; in early times only cathedrals could afford stained glass and in Canterbury Cathedral appears David seated, a crown on his head and a harp in his hands. This window dates back to c. 1178–1190. He appears in the same guise in the stained glass of York Minster, aged and crowned, with his harp. Another window in York represents him as the young shepherd fighting Goliath, a formidable figure in mediaeval armour. A brilliant but unknown sculptor has created a magnificent David which stands in the north transept of Chartres Cathedral. Another anonymous sculptor has carved a striking roof boss of King David the musician in Westminster Abbey. It dates from the mid-thirteenth century and is to be found in the west aisle of the north transept.

We see him again in the Westminster Psalter of the twelfth century; he is crowned and seated on a throne—a handsome king, playing his harp with beautifully positioned hands. The illumination has a variety of colours and expresses, both in David's face and in the whole composition, an appreciation of music and joy. There is a delightful picture in the Palacky University in Czechoslovakia; it dates from the thirteenth century and shows a young David, wearing a crown, surrounded by boys playing a variety of musical instruments.

Counted amongst the artists must be those illustrators who have, through the ages, decorated the Bible and Bible stories with pictures. These are so numerous that they remind us once more that for centuries many people could not read and learned of the Bible from pictures. Mention must be made of one of the most popular illustrated Bibles of all time: the Doré Bible of 1866. Perhaps the work of this brilliant French illustrator Gustave Doré (1833–1883) is not as famous now as it was at the end of the nineteenth century when London had its own Doré Gallery at 35 New Bond Street. At that time many children in Victorian families must have been frightened of hell-fire and a terrifying resurrection by their study—on Sundays—of the Doré Bible. The Doré Bible has a number of large woodcuts of the David story, notable ones being: 'David and Jonathan', and 'The Escape of David', showing Michal, his wife, lowering him from a window on a rope.

Neither is the story of David neglected in literature. We have George Peele's play *David and Bethsabe* sub-titled *The Love of a King*. Published in 1599, it is not a great work and describes events perhaps best forgotten. It was written and performed in the infancy of Elizabethan drama (Peele died in 1597) and is a crude, if sometimes effective, work.

The portrait of David in Dryden's satire: 'Absalom and Achitophel' is no more satisfactory but then the character is modelled on King Charles II and that monarch had little in common with the Psalmist.

More reverent treatment than either of these is the magnificent but obscure 'Song to David' by poor, crazy Christopher Smart (1722–1771) who spent most of his life in Bedlam. It is a sustained lyrical outburst in praise of the Psalmist and Poet. Smart also paraphrased the Psalms themselves, but these are of little merit and are deservedly forgotten.

Nor must we forget a play of modern times on the subject of the young David: Sir James Barrie's last play, *The Boy David* (1936). As a picture of boyhood, it is more effective than the more popular *Peter Pan*, but for some curious reason even the acting of Elisabeth Bergner (David), Godfrey Tearle (Saul), Sir John Martin-Harvey (Samuel) and the sets of Augustus John could not save it from being a commercial failure.

14

While talking about David and the stage, perhaps we should mention the glorious reading of the story of David and Goliath in a programme of Bible Readings toured in the USA by Charles Laughton just before his death in 1963. Fortunately for posterity, it has been recorded. The note of wonder in his voice in describing the size and equipment of Goliath is something not to be forgotten. Another great actor, Sir Laurence Olivier, has recorded a generous selection of Psalms for a long-playing record, with traditional music from Palestine.

7. David in History

Having considered David as a poet and a musician it would seem appropriate to survey briefly his equally important career as King and Soldier. In David's time, we are well out of the realms of Biblical legend and allegory and into a period when the Old Testament narrative relates undoubted historical fact. The story of David, the greatest of the Kings of Israel, is told in the two books of Samuel, which, until late in the history of our Bible, were one book. It relates a story of continual war with neighbouring tribes and internal strife. That David could unite a nation so war-torn was indeed a major achievement.

He was the son of Jesse, of the tribe of Judah, and an ancestor of Jesus. The youngest of eight sons, he spent his early life as a shepherd in the Bethlehem area at a time when his brothers were serving against the Philistines. He first found favour with Saul, first King of Israel, when he slew in somewhat unorthodox single combat, the Philistine champion, Goliath. Created King's armour-bearer for this deed, he further ingratiated himself with the Monarch by his musical abilities which calmed the melancholia verging on madness which afflicted Saul. Unfortunately, having aroused the jealousy of his unstable master, he was forced to flee the country and placed himself at the head of 400 outlaws with headquarters at the Cave of Adullam. For a period, for his own protection, he was a vassal of the King of Gath, a hereditary enemy of the Israelites.

After the death of Saul at Gilboa, David (who had been consecrated King by Samuel, the last of the Judges) ruled over Judah, while Saul's son, Ishbosheth, retained the rest of Israel. On his death, the whole of Israel came under

David's dominion. He conquered Jerusalem and made it the political and religious centre of the Kingdom, building for himself a palace on the highest of its hills, Mount Zion, where the Ark of the Covenant was also installed. After conquering the neighbouring tribes who had so long been a cause of trouble, he extended the Kingdom from Egypt to the Euphrates.

The last years of his reign were troubled by civil wars in which his two sons Absalom and Adonijah were implicated. But he created a powerful kingdom to which his son, Solomon, who succeeded him, was able to bring added prosperity. One of the great leaders of antiquity, his tragedy was that subsequent successions lacked the greatness to avert the waves of invasions which were to scatter the Jews.

8. Psalm 23: *Its popularity*

There is absolutely no doubt that the 23rd Psalm is the best known and best loved in the whole Psalter. Even the most prosaic translations cannot hide the fact that it is a lyric gem of great beauty and concentration.

It is one of those ascribed to King David and, from Biblical references, there can be no doubt of the poetical and musical gifts of the King. Not only could he play and compose music but he could write poetry and knew all about musical instruments. It would seem, therefore, a sound ascription. David is said to have reigned from about 1010 BC to about 970 BC and was therefore a near contemporary of Homer; so that this most finished work of art belongs to the period just before the infancy of Greek Classical literature.

9. Psalm 23: *Its imagery*

But let us now examine the reason why the 23rd Psalm must be considered such a sophisticated and perfect lyric poem. First of all, there is the striking imagery of the lines. What could be more expressive than the figurative description of death, which, in the hands of many writers, can become mawkish and morbid.

Dr John Brown, the Edinburgh physician and essayist, showed its true beauty when he used it in the passage describing the death of Old Ailie, the shepherd's wife, in

16

'Rab and his Friends' from *Horae Subsecivae* (1858–1862). The passage runs thus:

> 'She was walking alone through the valley of that shadow into which one day we must all enter—and yet she was not alone, for we all know whose rod and staff were comforting her.'

And what imagery can be more beautiful and more simple than 'green pastures' and 'still waters', the essence of peace? Since the psalm is written by a man who had, as we suppose, been a shepherd, the details of pastoral life are accurate and interesting. The allegory is also apt. God is described as one who looks after His people as the Shepherd looks after his sheep. This imagery appealed to the Hebrews as a pastoral people and Jesus became not only the Good Shepherd but the Holy Lamb of God; indeed, in many Victorian prayer books there is a photogravure frontispiece of Jesus as Shepherd with a crook carrying a lamb over His shoulder.

10. Psalm 23: a record of the Shepherd's life

But besides being poetical, the imagery is true to life. The 'green pastures' represent the fertile Wadi Fara, the only place in the arid Jordan area where there is green grass suitable for sheep, with still but clear and wholesome water where they may safely drink. Sheep choose their watering places with care since a fall into dangerous water may mean death by drowning when the fleece becomes sodden. They have apparently become aware of this and therefore have a fear of a doubtful watering place. 'The Valley of the Shadow of Death' is said to be a narrow, dangerous and terrifying passage among the mountains between Jerusalem and the Dead Sea where it requires a highly skilled man to lead flocks in safety.

11. Psalm 23: Allegory, Realism and Romanticism

It is also suggested by a modern writer on the 23rd Psalm (Rev. Ian Barclay in: *He is Everything to me—Thoughts on the 23rd Psalm*, 1972) that the work is autobiographical referring to the preservation of David during Absalom's rebellion through the loyalty of his mercenaries and the

17

subsequent arrival of much-needed supplies. Hence: 'The Lord is my Shepherd; I shall not want.' This is certainly not conclusive, but an interesting theory.

Besides the figurative use of the shepherd and his sheep, the poem describes a journey through life which gives it a wonderful artistic unity of subject. The traveller passes through pleasant and luscious parts until he comes to 'The Valley of the Shadow of Death', through which, like John Bunyan's Christian, he passes into eventual safety. Arriving at last at his destination, his Shepherd becomes his host, and the spiritual rewards of Heaven are described in terms of physical well-being—the lavish table where every attention is paid to the guest, and the promise of permanent happiness.

The Psalm is, in fact, a 'Pilgrim's Progress' in brief, and many of its readers may think it is not only David's auto-biography but also their own, just as they have identified themselves with Christian in Bunyan's book. One cannot help wondering if the Psalm was not the direct inspiration of his immortal allegory which treats the theme in so similar a manner. After accomplishing the journey through 'the Valley of the Shadow of Death', Christian meets with shepherds who help him on his journey to the Celestial City. Perhaps this, too, is significant.

Not only is the Psalm one of comfort and beauty, but it is a truly romantic poem in the same way as Wordsworth's poems are romantic: it gives an idealised but at the same time strictly accurate picture of pastoral life. Not only do we get true-to-life details about the safe pasturing of sheep but also of the equipment of the shepherd as Ian Barclay points out. We are told of his staff or crook, used to recapture straying sheep, and his rod or club, intended to defend them from the wild animals which abound in those areas. A crook has become a symbol of the care of God and is carried by bishops in the form of a crozier. Sometimes, indeed, they actually carry a real shepherd's crook.

12. Translations, paraphrases and parodies of Psalm 23
The 23rd Psalm has been translated with great frequency, paraphrased often, and sometimes parodied. Often it has appeared in dialect forms and the Scottish dialect is used in over twenty versions which have come into our possession.

That it is parodied may seem, at first sight, irreverent, but

18

it must be remembered that, to make a good parody, an author must study and thoroughly understand his original. This must show affection unless he is motivated by great dislike or hatred—which is, in this case, if not impossible, at least most unlikely.

That the psalm lends itself to dialect form shows that it is a homely, practical poem which applies to us all and which we can therefore fit into our own environment. A Dalesman, who translated a number of books of the Bible into his own dialect, said: 'Dialect is the very soul of a people.' The son of a Sussex farm labourer was 'a Methody local preecher for nigh on 50 years' and transcribed a number of 'Bits from de Old Book' into Sussex dialect because he wanted to show that the Good News could be put into simple language—which was how 'de Master' preached. A retired civil servant, who had published *The Gospels in Scouse'*, in collaboration with an Anglican clergyman, wrote a Liverpool version of Psalm 23, and to appreciate it one should ask a Liverpudlian to read it.

It is noteworthy that many versions which have reached us were written by shepherds—reminding us that the shepherd of David's day and the shepherd of our own day have much in common: thirty or so centuries do not really matter much.

Psalm 23 can be re-written in the familiar language of our own neighbourhood, or class of society, or in the language of our job or hobby, so that it has an immediate application to our life, surroundings and problems. The version on p. 115 written by a delinquent young man in an American prison may offend some. But should it offend? We suggest that readers try and understand Carl Burke's job, which was to get through to hostile or indifferent young people the real meaning of the Bible: he encouraged them to retell the Bible stories in their own 'hip' language. A shepherd meant literally nothing to them: a probation officer meant, probably, the first friend they had ever had.

13. Conclusion
The 23rd Psalm has led us—like many people before us—to consider a great range of subjects. The versions which we have selected and which fill the second part of this book will create a variety of new ideas in the minds of the readers. We

hope that our anthology will help people to feel in tune with David himself—with St Jerome—with the early translators, and the hymn writers, as well as with the scholars and thinkers of our own day.

It is worth remembering that the Book of Psalms was the only book of the Bible which mediaeval churches allowed their flocks to read uncensored.

We should like to quote from many of the writers whose books we enjoyed reading while we were compiling this anthology; but we will limit ourselves to two. We liked a quotation from Karl Barth in Thomas Merton's best-selling book *The Seven-Story Mountain*:

> 'The Bible gives to every man and to every era such answers to their questions as they deserve. We shall always find in it as much as we seek and no more—and nothing if it is nothing that we seek. . . .'

And Gelineau expressed his ideas thus:

> 'No one who takes the words of the psalms on his lips and their meaning in his heart, who allows the rhythm of their images to take hold of him and their accents to echo through his being, can possibly remain indifferent to them. . . . Inevitably they draw us beyond ourselves; they force us to that meeting with God without whom we cannot live and who transforms our whole life.'

In making our selection of versions we have had a curious feeling that time—nearly three millennia, and space—about 2000 miles as the crow flies—separating us from David have not held any importance. The one thing more important than time and space is that the Lord is our Shepherd, and that we shall not want.

PART II

Early Versions

HEBREW VERSION OF PSALM 23

מִזְמוֹר לְדָוִד

יְהוָה רֹעִי לֹא אֶחְסָר׃   בִּנְאוֹת דֶּשֶׁא יַרְבִּיצֵנִי

עַל־מֵי מְנֻחוֹת יְנַהֲלֵנִי׃   נַפְשִׁי יְשׁוֹבֵב

יַנְחֵנִי בְמַעְגְּלֵי־צֶדֶק לְמַעַן שְׁמוֹ׃ גַּם כִּי־אֵלֵךְ בְּגֵיא צַלְמָוֶת

לֹא־אִירָא רָע כִּי־אַתָּה עִמָּדִי   שִׁבְטְךָ וּמִשְׁעַנְתֶּךָ

הֵמָּה יְנַחֲמֻנִי׃   תַּעֲרֹךְ לְפָנַי ׀ שֻׁלְחָן נֶגֶד צֹרְרָי

דִּשַּׁנְתָּ בַשֶּׁמֶן רֹאשִׁי כּוֹסִי רְוָיָה׃   אַךְ ׀ טוֹב וָחֶסֶד יִרְדְּפוּנִי

כָּל־יְמֵי חַיָּי   וְשַׁבְתִּי בְּבֵית־יְהוָה לְאֹרֶךְ יָמִים׃

This is the original version and is thought to date back to David's time.

XXIII. A PSALM OF DAVID (from Young's *Literal Translation of the Bible*, 1862, modernised).

1   The Lord is my shepherd, I have no lack;

2   In pastures of tender grass
He causes me to lie down
By quiet waters He leads me.

3   My soul He refreshes;
He leads me in paths of righteousness
For His name's sake.

4   Also, when I walk in the valley of death-shade I fear
not evil;
For Thou *art* with me,
Thy rod and Thy staff—they comfort me.

5   Thou arrangest before me a table
Over-against my adversaries;
Thou hast anointed with oil my head;
My cup *is* full.

6   Only goodness and kindness pursue me
All the days of my life;
And my dwelling *is* in the house of the LORD for a
length of days.

THE VULGATE VERSION

Psalmus David XXII

1 Dominus regit me, & nihil mihi deerit.

2 In loco pascuae ibi me collocavit.
   Super aquam refectionis educavit me:

3 Animam meam convertit.
   Deduxit me super semitas justitiae, propter nomen
   suum

4 Nam & si ambulavero in medio umbrae mortis, non
   timebo mala; quoniam tu mecum es.
   Virga tua, & baculus tuus, ipsa me consolata sunt.

5 Parasti in conspectumeo mensam adversus eos, qui
   tribulant me.
   Impiguasti in oleo caput meum: & calix meus inebrians
   quam praeclarus est!

6 Et misericordia tua subsequetur ne omnibus diebus
   vitae meae.

7 Et ut inhabitem in domo Domini in longitudinem
   dierum.

This is taken from Biblia Sacra Vulgatae Editionis Rothomagi *1708, seen at Sussex University Library.*
   The authorised Latin Version of the Bible of the Roman Catholic Church was completed by St Jerome in AD *405. Jerome was born of Christian parents on the borders of Dalmatia (between 331 and 340). After years of penance and study and travel, he arrived in Rome in 382 and began his work on the Bible. Erasmus called Jerome: 'the Christian Cicero' because of the purity of his Latin. His version remains in use in the Roman church.*

The Lord gouerneth me, and no thing schal faile to me; in the place of pasture there he hath set me. He nurschide me on the watir of refreischyng; he conuertide my soule. He ledde me forth on the pathis of riʒtfulnesse; for his name. For whi thouʒ Y schal go in the myddis of schadewe of deeth; Y schal not drede yuels, for thou art with me. Thi ʒerde and thi staf: tho han coumfortid me. Thou hast maad redi a boord in my siʒt; aʒens hem that troblen me. Thou hast maad fat myn heed with oyle; and my cuppe, fillinge greetli, is ful cleer. And thi merci schal sue me; in alle the daies of my lijf. And that Y dwelle in the hows of the Lord; in to the lengthe of daies.

John Wycliffe (1320–1384) was a Fellow and subsequently Master of Balliol College, Oxford. He was early employed on a diplomatic mission to Bruges but sacrificed his political career to become leader of the Lollards, a movement which contained the germs of Protestantism. He founded an order of travelling priests to publicise his opinions and it was only due to the patronage of such powerful friends as the Duke of Lancaster and Lord Percy that the various charges of heresy laid against him failed. In 1428, his body was disinterred and thrown into the River Swift.

Wycliffe was among the earliest masters of English prose.

ANOTHER VERSION FROM THE WYCLIFFITE BIBLE

Probably by Nicholas de Hereford

The Lord gouerneth me and no thing to me shal lacke; in the place of leswe where he me ful sette. Ouer watir of fulfilling he nurshide me; my soule he conuertide. He broghte down upon me the sties of rightwiseness; for his name. For whi and if I shal go in the myddel of the shadowe of deth; I shal not dreden euelis, for thou art with me. Thi yerde and thi staf; the han confortid me. Thou hast maad redi in thi sighte a bord; agen them that trublyn me. Thou hast myche fatted in oile myn hed and my chalis makende ful drunken, hou right cler it is. And thi mercy shall vnderfolewe me; alle the dayis of my lif. And that I dwelle in the hous of the Lord in to the lengthe of dayis.

Nicholas de Hereford (active 1380–1417) was a student and fellow of Queen's College, Oxford; he preached continually in support of Wycliffe and the Lollards. He was excommunicated and imprisoned for a period but upon his release became leader of the Lollards after Wycliffe's death. Later recanting his heresies, he was appointed Chancellor and Treasurer of Hereford Cathedral and died a Carthusian monk at Coventry some time after 1417.

PSALM 23: IN THE COVERDALE BIBLE 1535

The Lorde is my shepherde I can want nothing. He fedeth
me in a greene pasture and ledeth me to a fresh water. He
quickeneth my soule and bringeth me forth in the ways of
righteousness for his names sake. Though I shulde walke
now in the valley of the shadowe of death yet I feare no
euell for thou art with me, thy staffe and thy shepehoke
comforte me.
Thou preparest a table before me agaynst mine enemies thou
anoyntest my heade with oyle and fyllest my cuppe full.
Oh let thy louingkyndness and mercy followe me all the
dayes of my lyfe that I may dwell in the house of the Lord
for euer.

*Miles Coverdale (1488–1568) was an English clergyman of
advanced Lutheran views who became a friend of Thomas Cromwell.
His translation of the Bible published in Zurich owed much to
Tyndale. His translation of the Psalms was incorporated into the
Book of Common Prayer. Bishop of Exeter in 1551, he was ejected
under Queen Mary in 1553. He returned to the continent where
he remained until 1559. He was appointed Vicar of St Magnus,
London Bridge, in 1564, but was forced to retire in 1566 on
account of his pronounced Puritan views.*

VERSION IN THE FIRST BOOK OF COMMON PRAYER 1549

Psalm 23   *Dominus regit me*

The Lorde is my shepheard: therefore can I lacke nothing.

He shal feede me in a greene pasture: and leade me foorth beside the waters of comfort.

He shal conuert my soule: and bring me forth in the pathes of righteousnes for his names sake.

Yea though I walke thorow the valley of the shadowe of death, I wil feare no euil: for thou art with me, thy rod and thy staffe comfort me.

Thou shalt prepare a table before me against them that trouble me: thou hast anoynted my head with oyle, and my cup shalbe full.

But thy louingkindnesse and mercy shall follow me all the dayes of my life: and I will dwell in the house of the Lorde for euer.

The Psalms are based on the translations of Tyndale (1525) and Miles Coverdale (1535) (see p. 27 of this book). The Prayer Book was first issued in the reign of Edward VI and was mainly the work of Thomas Cranmer, Archbishop of Canterbury. The Prayer Book has been several times revised, notably in 1662 and 1927.

William Tyndale (c. 1492–1536) was educated at Oxford and Cambridge and helped to introduce the 'New Learning' into England by translating works by Erasmus. For this, he was publicly rebuked. He left for Germany where he met Luther, and commenced his translation of the Bible at Cologne. When he was prevented from continuing by injunction, he completed it at Worms. He was denounced as a heretic by Cardinal Wolsey and was, after many adventures and escapes, arrested by the Imperial Officers. After strangulation his body was burned.

William Tyndale has this to say about the art of translation: addressing himself to his 'better equipped readers' he says:

> *'If they perceive in any places that I have not attained the very sense of the tongue, or meaning of the Scripture, or have not given the right word, that they put their hands to amend it, remembering that so is their duty to do. . . .'*

A RHYMED VERSION BY W.W. (*16th century*)

The Lord is only my support,
 and he that doth me feed:
How can I then lack any thing
 whereof I stand in need?
In pastures green he feedeth me
 where I do safely lie:
And after leads me to the streams
 which run most pleasantly.
And when I find myself near lost
 then doth he me home take,
Conducting me in his right paths
 even for his own Name's sake.
And though I were e'en at death's door,
 yet would I fear no ill,
For both thy rod and shepherd's crook
 afford me comfort still.
Thou hast my table richly deckt
 in presence of my foe:
Thou hast my head with balm refresht,
 my cup doth overflow.
And finally while breath doth last
 thy grace shall me defend:
And in the house of God will I
 my life for ever spend.

W.W. was William Whittingham (*1524–1579*), *a Puritan Fellow of All Souls College, Oxford, who fled to Geneva to escape the Marian persecutions. He was one of the main translators of the Geneva (Breeches) Bible (1556–1557) and assisted with Kethe's Geneva Psalter (1561). In addition, he produced metrical versions of the Psalms and Ten Commandments.*

Returning to England in 1560, he became Dean of Durham in 1563. In 1578, he was charged with invalidity of his ordination but died before the accusation could be proved.

PSAL XXIII IN METRE BY T.S.

1   My shepeheard is the living Lord,
      Nothing therefore I need:
    In pastures fair with waters calme,
      He sets me forth to feede.

2   He did conuert and glad my soule,
      And brought my mind in frame;
    To walke in pathes of righteousnesse,
      For his most holy name.

3   Yea though I walke in vale of death
      Yet will I feare none ill:
    Thy rod, thy staffe, do comfort me,
      And thou art with me still.

4   And in the presence of my foes,
      My table thou shalt spread:
    Thou shalt, O Lord, fill full my cup,
      And eke anoint my heade.

5   Through all my life thy fauour is,
      so franckly shewed to me:
    That in thy house for euermore,
      My dwelling place shall be.

Thomas Sternhold (1500–1549) was Groom of the Chamber to Henry VIII and Edward VI. His first translation of Selected Psalms was published in 1549. The Complete Psalter with his and John Hopkins' translations appeared in 1562.

This is hymn no. 356 in the Church Hymnal (1917); the fourth verse above is usually omitted.

PSAL XXIII IN THE BREECHES BIBLE

Because the Prophet had prooued the great mercies of God at diuers times, and in sundry maners, hee gathereth a certain assurance, fully persuading himselfe that God will continue the uery same goodnesse towards him for euer.

A PSALME OF DAUID

The Lord is my shepheard, I shall not want.

He maketh mee to rest in greene pasture, and leadeth me by the still waters.

Hee restoreth my soule, and leadeth me in the paths of righteousnesse for his Names sake.

Yea, though I should walke through the valley of the shadowe of death, I will feare no euill: for thou art with me: thy rod and thy staffe, they comfort me.

Thou doest prepare a table before me in the sight of mine aduersaries: thou doest anoynt mine head with oile, and my cup runneth ouer.

Doubtlesse kindnesse, and mercie shall followe mee all the dayes of my life, and I shall remaine a long season in the house of the Lord.

The Breeches Bible is another name for the Geneva Bible and was first brought out in 1556/7. It is called the Breeches Bible from the translation of Genesis iii :7 : 'They sewed fig leaves together and made themselves breeches.'

The translators were Puritan reformers who had fled from the persecution of Mary Tudor ; William Whittingham was one of the major translators.

The above version appeared in a 1578 edition. Moralising to aid the clergy appeared in the margins.

A facsimile of the 1560 edition was published by Madison, University of Wisconsin Press, in 1969.

1   God is my shephearde therefore I can lacke nothyng: he wyll cause me to repose myselfe in pasture full of grasse and he wyll leade me vnto calme waters.

2   He will conuert my soule: he wyll bring me foorth into the pathes of righteousnesse for his names sake.

3   Yea though I walke through the valley of the shadowe of death I wyll fear no euyll: for thou art with me, thy rodde and thy staffe be the thynges that do comfort me.

4   Thou wilt prepare a table before me in the presence of myne aduersaries: thou has anoynted my head with oyle and my cup shalbe brumme ful.

5   Truly felicitie and mercy shal folowe me all the dayes of my lyfe: and I wyll dwell in the house of God for a long tyme.

The Bishops' Bible was a revision of the Great Bible of 1539. It has been described as a 'backward looking Bible' since it lost the musical diction of its original and gained no greater accuracy.

DOMINUS REGIT ME

The Lord, the Lord my shepherd is,
  And so can never I
    Tast missery.
He rests me in greene pasture his:
  By waters still, and sweete
    Hee guides my feete.

Hee me revives: leades me the way,
  Which righteousnesse doth take.
    For his names sake.
Yea though I should through valleys stray,
  Of deathes dark shade, I will
    Noe whitt feare ill.

For thou, deere Lord, thou me besett'st:
  Thy rodd, and thy staff be
    To comfort me;
Before me thou a table sett'st,
  Even when foes envious ey
    Doth it espy.

Thou oil'st my head, thou fill'st my cupp:
  Nay more thou endlesse good,
    Shalt give me food.
To thee, I say, ascended up,
  Where thou, the Lord of all,
    Dost hold thy hall.

Sir Philip Sidney (1554–1586) and Mary Herbert, Countess of Pembroke (1561–1621) collaborated in a complete Psalter. Sidney shone in everything he touched: soldier, diplomat, courtier, critic (Defence of Poesie *1595*), *poet* (Astrophel and Stella etc. *1580*), *romantic novelist* (Arcadia *1590*). *His heroic death at the Battle of Zutphen in the Netherlands against the Spaniards made him a national hero.*

His sister, Mary, Countess of Pembroke, suggested to him the writing of Arcadia *and revised and edited it after his death. She was the patroness of Ben Jonson, Samuel Daniel, Nicholas Breton and other poets of the period.*

J. C. A. Rathmel edited The Psalms of Sir Philip Sidney and the Countess of Pembroke (*New York, Doubleday 1963*).

Seventeenth-Century Versions

PSALM 22 (23) IN THE DOUAI BIBLE (1609–1610)

Dominus regit me
God's spiritual benefits to faithful souls

A Psalm for David

The Lord ruleth me; and I shall want nothing.

He hath set me in a place of pasture.

He hath brought me up on the water of refreshment:
he hath converted my soul.

He hath led me on the paths of justice,
for his own name's sake.

For though I should walk in the midst of the shadow of
death I will fear no evils; for thou art with me.

Thy rod and thy staff: they have comforted me.

Thou hast prepared a table before me against them that
afflict me.

Thou hast anointed my head with oil: and my chalice which
inebriateth me, how goodly is it!

And thy mercy will follow me all the days of my life:

And that I may dwell in the house of the Lord unto length
of days.

*The Douai Bible is a Roman Catholic version in English and
became an important publication in the Counter-Reformation.
The New Testament appeared in Rheims in 1582 and the Old
Testament in Douai 1600–1610.*

PSALM 23 IN THE AUTHORISED VERSION OF THE BIBLE 1611

David's confidence in God's grace

The Lord is my shepherd; I shall not want.
He maketh me to lie down in green pastures:
he leadeth me beside the still waters.

He restoreth my soul: he leadeth me in the paths
of righteousness for his name's sake.

Yea, though I walk through the valley
of the shadow of death, I will fear no evil:
for thou art with me; thy rod and thy staff
they comfort me.

Thou preparest a table before me
in the presence of mine enemies: thou anointest
my head with oil; my cup runneth over.

Surely goodness and mercy shall follow me
all the days of my life: and I will dwell
in the house of the LORD for ever.

This version arose out of the Hampton Court Conference, called by James I in 1604 at the request of the Puritans to reform the English Church. No point of agreement was reached beyond the proposal for a new translation of the Bible and consequently the production of the best loved translation of the 23rd Psalm.

PSALM 23

Taken from the Book of Psalms by Henry Ainsworth

Iehovah feedeth me, I shall not lack.

In grassy folds, he down douth make me lye:
he gently-leads me, quiet waters by. He dooth return my
soul: for his name sake, in paths of justice leads-me-quietly.

Yea, though I walk, in dale of deadly-shade,
ile fear none yll; for with me thou wilt be:
thy rod thy staff eke, they shall comfort me.

Fore me, a table thou hast read-made;
in their presence that my distressers be:

Thou makes-fat mine head with oincling oil;
my cup abounds.

Doubtless, good and mercie shall all the dayes of my life
folow me: also within Jehovahs howse I shall to length of
dayes, repose-me-quietlie.

*This version appears in an old Bible belonging to the Earl of
Harrowby at Sandon Hall, Stafford. The book was printed in
Amsterdam in 1622 and was probably printed by a Dutchman
who was not certain about English rhymes, hyphens etc.*
    *Henry Ainsworth (1571–1623) was leader of the Separatist
Congregation at Amsterdam. He started as a bookseller's porter,
but subsequently became leader of the Francis Johnson Church.
He was the author of many learned theological works—now rare.
In the early seventeenth century there were many English non-
conformists who settled in Holland to gain freedom of worship.*

PSALM 23

From a Bible in the Harrowby Trust Library

Iehovah feedeth me, I shall not lack. In folds of budding-
grass, he maketh me lie down: he easily-leadeth me,
by the waters of rest.

He returneth my soul: he leadeth me in the beaten-paths of
justice, for his name sake.

Yea, though I should walk in the valley of the shade of death,
I will not fear evil; for thou wilt be with me:
Thy rod and thy staff, they shal comfort me.

Thou furnishest before me, a table; in presence of my
distressers: thou makest fat my head with oil; my cup
is abundant.

Doubtless, good and mercy shal folow me, al the dayes of
my life: & I shal converse in the howse of Iehovah,
to length of dayes.

PSALM 23

From the BOOK OF PRAYSES CALLED THE PSALMES, *the* KEYES *and Holly things of* DAVID

XXIII   A Psalme of David

THE ETERNALL is my sheaperd, I shall not want, he will fold me vpon the greene gresse, and leade me by the quyet waters. Hee will couvert my minde, and guyde mee in the tracks of RIGHTEOUSNESS, for his Names sake.

Yea when I goe in the dim & dusky valley, I feare no ill, because thou art with me, and thy very rodd & thy leaning staff, they comfort me,
hard by my tormenters thou furnishest a table before me.

Thou anointest my head with oyle, and fillest my Cupp brim full, for goodnes and KINDENES have followed mee all dayes of my life, and I will contynwe in the House of the ETERNALL to my lives end.

This version appeared in THE BOOK OF PRAYSES . . . According to the Letter, and the Mystery of them. AND According to the rule and Methode of the Compile-er . . . *by Alexander Top Esquier.*
The book was printed in 'Amstelredam' *by Ian Frederick z Stam in 1629. (The printer was probably a Dutchman who made minor misprints, e.g. couvert for convert, thy for they.)*

THE VERSION OF GEORGE HERBERT

The God of love my Shepherd is,
   And he that doth me feed;
While he is mine and I am his,
   What can I want or need?

He leads me to the tender grass,
   Where I both feed and rest;
Then to the streams that gently pass:
   In both I have the best.

Or if I stray, he doth convert,
   And bring my mind in frame,
And all this for my desert,
   But for his holy name.

Yea, in death's shady black abode,
   Well may I walk, not fear;
For thou art with me, and thy rod
   To guide, thy staff to bear.

Nay, Thou dost make me sit and dine
   Ev'n in my enemies' sight:
My head with oyl, my cup with wine
   Runnes over day and night.

Surely thy sweet and wondrous love
   Shall measure all my days;
And, as it never shall remove,
   So neither shall my praise.

George Herbert (1593–1633) was one of the greatest seventeenth-century devotional poets. He deserted the Court for the Vicarage of Bemerton, near Salisbury. His main poetical output is in The Temple (1633) *and it is in this book that the above version appears.*

   Herbert's life was written by his friend Izaak Walton, author of The Compleat Angler.

The Lord's my Shepherd, I'll not want.
He makes me down to lie
In pastures green: he leadeth me
The quiet waters by.

My soul he doth restore again
And me to walk doth make
Within the paths of righteousness
Ev'n for his own name's sake.

Yea, tho' I walk in death's dark vale
Yet will I fear none ill:
For thou art with me: and thy rod
And staff me comfort still.

My table thou hast furnished
In presence of my foes;
My head thou dost with oil anoint
And my cup overflows.

Goodness and mercy all my life
Shall surely follow me
And in God's house for evermore
My dwelling-place shall be.

*Francis Rous (1579–1659) was a Puritan and one time M.P. for
Truro, standing in the Short and the Long Parliaments. He was
a member of Cromwell's Council of State and Provost of Eton; he
was also the author of many theological works.*

*William Barton (1603–1678) was believed to have been that
Barton who was Vicar of Mayfield, Staffs. He published a
Century of Select Hymns as well as a verse translation of
the Psalms.*

*The above version was revised for the Scottish Psalter in 1650
and again for the General Assembly of the Church of Scotland in
1696. It is sung to the tune of Crimond.*

It is hymn no. 355 in the Church Hymnal.

THE VERSION OF TATE AND BRADY

The Lord himself, the mighty Lord, vouchsafes to be my
    guide;
The Shepherd by whose constant care my wants are all
    supply'd.

In tender grass he makes me feed, and gently there repose;
Then leads me to cool shades, and where refreshing water
    flows.

He does my wand'ring soul reclaim, and, to his endless
    praise,
Instruct with humble zeal to walk in his most righteous ways.

I pass the gloomy vale of death from fear and danger free:
For there his aiding rod and staff defend and comfort me.

In presence of my spiteful foes he does my table spread;
He crowns my cup with cheerful wine, with oil anoints my
    head.

Since God does thus his wondrous love through all my life
    extend,
That life to him I will devote, and in his temple spend.

*Nahum Tate (1652–1715) and Nicholas Brady (1659–1726):
Nahum Tate was Poet Laureate from 1690. He re-wrote* King
Lear *with a happy ending and this version held the stage until
the nineteenth century. He was said by a contemporary to have
'been a man of intemperate and improvident life'.*

    *He produced his Metrical Psalter with Nicholas Brady in 1695.
Brady was a pluralist Parson of the Church of England, holding
the livings of Stratford-upon-Avon, Richmond and Clapham.*

Eighteenth-Century Versions

A VERSION BY ISAAC WATTS

The Lord my shepherd is,
I shall be well supplied;
Since he is mine and I am his,
What can I want beside?

He leads me to the place
Where heavenly pasture grows,
Where living waters gently pass,
And full salvation flows.

If e'er I go astray,
He doth my soul reclaim;
And guides me in his own right way,
For his most holy name.

While he affords his aid
I cannot yield to fear;
Though I should walk through death's dark shade
My shepherd's with me there.

In spite of all my foes,
Thou dost my table spread;
My cup with blessings overflows,
And joy exalts my head.

The bounties of thy love
Shall crown my following days;
Nor from thy house will I remove,
Nor cease to speak thy praise.

*Isaac Watts (1674–1748) was a nonconformist minister and a
popular preacher. He spent the greater part of his life as domestic
chaplain to Sir Thomas Abney at Theobalds. (Sir Thomas Abney
was one of the promoters and directors of the Bank of England.
Besides being a benefactor of St Thomas's Hospital he was elected
Lord Mayor of London 1700–1701.)*

The following is an extract from the advertisement of the 1718 edition of his Psalms of David; *this book contains the complete Psalter, many of the psalms being in several versions:*

> 'The chief design of this work was to improve psalmody, or religious singing and to encourage the frequent passage of it in public assemblies and private families with more honour and delight; yet the Author hopes that the reading of it may also entertain the parlour and the closet with devout pleasure and holy meditations. Therefore he would request his readers at proper seasons to peruse it through; and among three hundred suit their own case and temper, or the circumstances of their families and friends; they may teach their children such as are proper for their age; and by treasuring them in their memory they may be furnished for pious retirement, or may entertain their friends with holy melody.'

Watts' life is included (along with that of Addison) in Dr Johnson's Lives of the Poets.

CHARLES WESLEY'S VERSION

From John Wesley's Hymn-Book 1779

Jesus the good shepherd is;
Jesus died the sheep to save.
He is mine and I am His
All I want in Him I have,
Life and health and rest and food,
All the plenitude of God.

Jesus loves and guards His own
Me in verdant pastures feeds,
Makes me quietly lie down;
By the streams of comfort leads;
Following Him where'er He goes,
Silent joy my heart o'erflows.

He in sickness makes me whole,
Guides me into paths of peace,
He revives my fainting soul,
Stablishes in righteousness;
Who for me vouchsafed to die;
Loves me still, I know not why!

Unappalled by guilty fear,
Through the mortal vale I go;
My eternal life is near;
Thee my life in death I know;
Bless thy cheering, chastening rod;
Die into the arms of God.

Till that welcome hour I see,
Thou before my foe dost flee;
Bidst me sit and feed with thee,
Pour'st thy oil upon my head;
Giv'st me all I ask and more,
Mak'st my cup of joy run o'er.

Love divine shall still embrace,
Love shall keep me to the end;
Surely all my happy days,
I shall in thy temple spend,
Till I to thy House remove
Thy eternal house above!

Charles Wesley (1707–1788) with his brother John, was one of the founders of the Methodist movement, 1738–1739. He was the poet of the movement, and he wrote 6500 hymns. They are of unequal merit but some are among the best in the language.

A VERSION FROM
THE PSALMS AND OTHER PASSAGES OF
SCRIPTURE

*Translated or imitated and adapted as Select Hymns
to Christian Worship*

GOD OUR SHEPHERD

Lo! my Shepherd's Hand divine!
Want shall never more be mine.
In a Pasture fair and large
He shall feed his happy Charge;
And my Couch with tend'rest Care,
'Midst the springing Grass prepare.
When I faint with summer's Heat,
He shall lead my weary Feet
To the Streams that still and slow
Through the verdant Meadow flow.

He my Soul anew shall frame
And, his Mercy to proclaim,
When thro' devious Paths I stray,
Teach my steps the better Way.
Tho' the dreary Vale I tread,
By the Shades of Death o'erspread,
There I walk from Terror free,
While my every Wish I see
By Thy Rod and Staff supplied;
This my Guard, and that my Guide.

While my Foes are gazing on,
Thou thy fav'ring Care hast shown;
Thou my plenteous Board hast spread,
Thou, with Oil refresh'd my Head;
Fill'd by Thee my Cup o'erflows;
For Thy Love no Limit knows;
Constant to my latest End
This my Footsteps shall attend,
And shall bid Thy hallow'd Dome
Yield me an eternal Home.

This hymn was in a book printed in Lewes in 1784. The version is the same as one published in Improved Psalmody *published by the Reverend James Merrick in 1784.*

The version printed above was seen in a book presented to Lewes Museum; it bears on the flyleaf: 'Mr Ellman's seat'. Mr Ellman (1753–1832) was a well-known local breeder of Southdown sheep.

The Lord my pasture shall prepare,
And feed me with a shepherd's care;
His presence shall my wants supply,
And guard me with a watchful eye;
My noonday walks he shall attend,
And all my midnight hours defend.

When in the sultry glebe I faint,
Or on the thirsty mountain pant,
To fertile vales and dewy meads,
My weary wandering steps he leads,
Where peaceful rivers, soft and slow,
Amid the verdant landscape flow.

Though in the paths of death I tread,
With gloomy horrors overspread,
My steadfast heart shall fear no ill,
For thou, O Lord, art with me still;
Thy rod and staff shall give me aid,
And guide me through the dreadful shade.

Tho' in a bare and rugged Way,
Through devious lonely Wilds I stray,
Thy Bounty shall my Pains beguile:
The barren Wilderness shall smile
With sudden Greens and Herbage crown'd,
And Streams shall murmur all around.

Joseph Addison (1672–1719) was essayist, dramatist, poet and politician. He is most famous for his periodical: The Spectator *in which appeared the* De Coverley Papers *and the above translation version of Psalm 23 (Essay 441). Of his plays* Cato *is the best and it held the stage until the end of the eighteenth century.*

Many of Addison's Essays were in effect sermons and Essay 441 is a sermon with Psalm 23 as its theme. He concludes: 'David has very beautifully represented this steady Reliance on God Almighty in his twenty-third Psalm, which is a kind of Pastoral Hymn, and filled with those Allusions which are usual in that kind of writing. The Poetry is very exquisite. . . .'

The above hymn is no. 356 in the Church Hymnal; the fourth verse is usually omitted.

Nineteenth-Century Versions

A POETICAL VERSION OF PSALM XXIII

My Shepherd is the Lord of life,
  What can his creature need?
Sweet is the spring I drink and green
  The pasture where I feed.

My soul he shall convert and keep
  My wand'ring steps in sight,
And for the honor of his name
  Direct their course aright.

Yea, to the dark and shadowy vale
  Of death though I repair,
Thy rod and thy supporting staff
  Shall be my comfort there.

In presence of the envious foe
  My table thou hast spread;
Wine thou bestow'st to fill my cup
  And oyl to deck my head.

I know thy mercy shall endure
  Till life itself shall cease,
And evermore with Thee I'll dwell
  In holiness and peace.

Richard Cumberland (1732–1811), known as the 'Terence of England', was a dramatist and novelist who lived many years in Tunbridge Wells. His novels and tragedies are forgotten but the best of his sentimental comedies—'The Jew' and 'The West Indian'—are still read. He figures as Sir Fretful Plagiary in Sheridan's 'The Critic', and was eminent enough to be buried in Westminster Abbey.

His Poetical Versions of the Psalms *appeared in 1801.*

The Lord is my Shepherd,
No want shall I know;
I feed in green pastures,
Safe folded I rest;
He leadeth my soul where
The still waters flow,
Restores me when wand'ring,
Redeems when oppressed.

Thro' the valley and shadow
Of death though I stray,
Since Thou art my guardian,
No evil I fear;
Thy rod shall defend me,
Thy staff be my stay;
No harm can befall with
My Comforter near.

In midst of affliction
My table is spread,
With blessings unmeasured
My cup runneth o'er;
With perfume and oil Thou
Anointest my head,
O what shall I ask
Of Thy providence more?

Let goodness and mercy,
My bountiful God,
Still follow my steps
Till I meet Thee above;
I seek by the path
Which my forefathers trod
Through the land of their sojourn
Thy kingdom of Love.

James Montgomery (1771–1854) was a radical journalist and philanthropist. He served three years in York gaol for sedition. He became a moderate Conservative in 1825 and received a pension from Sir Robert Peel. Apart from his hymns, his poems are forgotten.

My shepherd is the Lord: I know
  No care or craving need:
He lays me where the green herbs grow
  Along the quiet mead:

He leads me where the waters glide,
  The waters soft and still,
And homeward He will gently guide
  My wandering heart and will.

He brings me on the righteous path,
  Even for His Name's dear sake.
What if in vale and shade of Death
  My dreary way I take?

I fear no ill, for Thou, O God,
  With me for ever art;
Thy shepherd's staff, Thy guiding rod,
  'Tis they console my heart.

For me Thy board is richly spread
  In sight of all my foes,
Fresh oil of Thine embalms my head,
  My cup of grace o'erflows.

O nought but love and mercy wait
  Through all my life on me,
And I within my Father's gate
  For long bright years shall be.

This version appears in John Keble's Psalter in English Verse, in an edition with an introduction by the Archbishop of Armagh. Keble (1792–1866) was a High Church clergyman, involved in the Oxford Movement. His Christian Year (1828) was the most popular devotional work of the century. He was Vicar of Hursley, Hants, a Fellow of Oriel College and Oxford Professor of Poetry. His metrical version of the Psalms never became popular.
  Keble College, Oxford, is his memorial.

THE VERSION OF HORATIUS BONAR:
A FREE RENDERING

Under Thy shadow,
   Shepherd and King,
Safe from all evil
   Under Thy wing.
Strangers and pilgrims,
   Forward we move,
Calm in Thy keeping,
   Strong in Thy love.

Leaning upon Thee,
   Close by Thy side,
In Thy communion,
   We would abide.
Closer still clinging,
   Saviour, to Thee,
Daily our journey
   Upwards shall be.

Goodness and mercy
   Ever attend,
Guidance and keeping
   On to the end!
Solace in sorrow,
   Brightness in gloom,
Light everlasting
   Over the tomb!

Counsel and comfort,
   Whate'er befall,
Thou will afford us,
   Saviour, in all.
Let Thy glad presence
   Still with us dwell:
Nothing shall harm us,
   All shall be well.

Faint yet pursuing,
   Upwards we rise;
See the bright city,
   Yonder the prize!
On to the haven,
   To the calm shore,
In the fair city
   Safe evermore!

Horatius Bonar (1808–1889) was a Scottish divine who, after mission work at Leith and a ministry at Kelso, joined the Free Church (1843). He became Minister at the Chalmers Memorial Church, Edinburgh, in 1866, and Moderator of the General Assembly of Free Churches in 1883. Among his many hymns are: 'I heard the voice of Jesus say. . . .'

The above hymn appeared in Everybody's Psalm, *published in 1947.*

The King of love my Shepherd is,
Whose goodness faileth never;
I nothing lack if I am His
And He is mine for ever.

Where streams of living water flow
My ransom'd soul He leadeth,
And, where the verdant pastures grow,
With food celestial feedeth.

Perverse and foolish oft I strayed,
But yet in love He sought me,
And on His Shoulder gently laid,
And home, rejoicing, brought me.

In death's dark vale I fear no ill
With Thee, dear Lord, beside me;
Thy rod and staff my comfort still,
Thy Cross before to guide me.

Thou spread'st a Table in my sight;
Thy Unction grace bestoweth;
And oh, what transport of delight
From Thy pure Chalice floweth!

And so through all the length of days
Thy goodness faileth never:
Good Shepherd, may I sing Thy praise
Within Thy house for ever.

Sir Henry Williams Baker (1821–1877) was Vicar of Monkland, near Leominster, from 1851. He edited and promoted The Hymns Ancient and Modern *and these were published in 1861. 'The King of Love my Shepherd is' was first published in the Appendix of the first edition, no. 330. It remains today one of the best-known of the hymns and is selected more than any other for services on special occasions; it was one of the two hymns sung at the funeral of the Duke of Windsor.*

The Rev. John Ellerton (himself a hymn-writer) says that the third verse of this hymn was Sir Henry Baker's last recorded utterance.

This hymn is now no. 197 in Hymns Ancient and Modern *and no. 202 in the* Church Hymnal.

A METRICAL VERSION OF THE TWENTY-THIRD PSALM

By W. S. Passmore and Henry Smart

The LORD is my Shepherd, I never shall want,
  For lack of His mercy my soul shall not pant:
  In pleasant green pastures I daily abide,
  He leads me the peaceful still waters beside.

My soul He restoreth, and for His Name's sake
  The path of true righteousness bids me to take:
  Yea, though I walk through Death's dark valley and shade
  I will not by evil be ever dismayed.

For Thou are my Shepherd, and with me alway
  Thy rod and Thy staff are my comfort and stay:
  Thy table Thou spreadest in presence of foes,
  My head Thou anointest, my cup overflows.

Thy goodness and mercy shall follow me still,
  While life's earnest duty I daily fulfil;
  Till, joyous, my spirit shall claim its Reward
  And dwell evermore in the House of the Lord.

W. S. Passmore and Henry Smart (1813–1879). Henry Smart who composed the music to this version of the 23rd Psalm, translated by W. S. Passmore (about whom we have been able to discover no further information) was intended for the Army, but on refusing a commission in India, trained as a solicitor. Deserting this for music, he became an organist at several London churches. He composed both sacred and secular music, including an opera, and wrote musical criticism for the press.

    His setting for Passmore's version of the 23rd Psalm is still in print as an octavo music sheet.

PARAPHRASE OF 23RD PSALM

By Rev. Thomas Edwards

In pastures green, dear Shepherd, lead
A weary sheep of Thine,
In pastures rich, I fain would feed,
This hungry soul of mine.

Oh, make me with Thy flock lie down
Where Thy still waters flow
Where pardon, peace and love abound
And fruits celestial grow.

When Jordan's swelling waves appear,
Hold Thou my trembling hand;
No evil let Thy servant fear
But firm in Jesus stand.

The Gospel 'rod' reveal to me
Thy 'staff' of promise strong;
In all its fullness let me see
My Hope, my Shield, my Song.

Let Goodness, Lord, and mercy, too
For ever follow me;
Till I Thy face in glory view;
Till I Thy glory see.

Oh, then with me it shall be well
When in Thy house above,
I shall for ever, ever dwell
And sing redeeming love.

Thomas Edwards (1817–1893) gave up being a butcher and became first a Baptist Minister and later an independent minister at his own chapel, Salem, in Tunbridge Wells. Extremely evangelistic, his open-air services on the Common became famous. He wrote numerous psalms and hymns (of no great merit); selections were published in Waters in the Wilderness *(1876) and* Nature Poems *(1893).*

Jesus my Shepherd my want shall supply:
　　Down in green pastures He makes me to lie;
He leads me beside the still waters of rest;
　　My soul He restores to the fold of the blest.

If from His paths I am tempted to stray,
　　He guards me from sin, and guides in the way;
I walk undismayed through the valley of dread,
　　Where darkness and death gather over my head.

Evil I fear not, for with me Thou art;
　　Thy rod and Thy staff, they comfort my heart;
Thou spreadest my table in sight of my foes;
　　My head Thou anointest, my cup overflows.

Goodness and mercy shall follow me still
　　All my life long, as my course I fulfil;
Then, Saviour, for ever, in heaven above,
　　With Thee I shall dwell, in the home of Thy love.

*This version appears in the Methodist Hymn Book, 1904,
number 395. Judge Waddy (1830–1902) was trained as a
clergyman but before ordination went to the Bar. He became a
noted Queen's Counsel, and was Judge of the Sheffield Circuit.
He was a popular lay preacher.*

A VERSION FROM ST OLAVE'S HYMNARY 1898

He leadeth me   Psalm 23

In pastures green? Not always; sometimes He
Who knoweth best, in kindness leadeth me
In weary ways, where heavy shadows be.

Out of the sunshine, warm and soft and bright—
Out of the sunshine into darkest night;
I oft would faint, with sorrow and affright—

Only for this I know—He holds my hand,
So whether in the green or desert land,
I trust, although I may not understand.

And by still waters? No, not always so;
Oft-time the heavy tempests round me blow,
And o'er my soul the waves and billows go.

But when the storms beat loudest, and I cry
Aloud for help the Master standeth by,
And whispers to my soul, 'Lo, it is I'.

Above the tempest wild I hear Him say—
'Beyond this darkness lies the perfect day.
In every path of thine I lead the way.'

So, whether on the hilltops high and fair
I dwell, or in the sunless valleys, where
The shadows lie—what matters—He is there.

And more than this; where'er the pathway lead
He gives to me no helpless, broken reed,
But His Own Hand, sufficient for my need.

So where He leads me, I can safely go,
And in the blest hereafter I shall know
Why in His Wisdom He hath led me so.

The St Olave's Hymnary was compiled by W. G. Rushbrooke, Headmaster of St Olave's and St Saviour's Grammar School, Orpington, 1893–1922. Mr Rushbrooke was a distinguished Biblical scholar, and a notable headmaster in his day. The hymnary was in use up to 1939, and we are told that Old Boys retain a considerable affection for it. Composer of this version unknown.

THE TEACHER PSALM

By Henry van Dyke

The Lord is my Teacher; I shall not lose the way.
He leadeth me in the lowly paths of learning.
He prepareth a lesson for me every day.
He bringeth me to the clear fountains of instruction;
Little by little He showeth me the beauty of truth.

He taketh me by the hand to the hill-top of vision
And my soul is glad when I perceive His meaning.
In the valley He also walketh beside me,
In the dark places He whispereth to my soul.

Even though my lesson be hard, it is not hopeless.
For the Lord is patient with His slow scholar.
He will wait awhile for my weakness,
And help me to read the truth through tears.

Henry van Dyke (1852–1933) was an American Presbyterian clergyman and also an author, an educationist and diplomat. He was Murray Professor of English Literature at Princeton University from 1899–1923, U.S. Minister to the Netherlands and Luxembourg from 1913 to 1916. Among his numerous writings was a study of the poetry of Tennyson, but he is more famous for his religious study The Story of the Other Wise Man, *which was first delivered as a sermon.*

Twentieth-Century Versions

PSALM 23 FROM HOLY BIBLE IN MODERN
ENGLISH

My Lord attends;—I shall not want:
He lets me rest in verdant fields,
He leads me by the pleasant brooks,
He brings me back, my life refreshed.

Though I may walk through Death's dark Vale,
I fear no hurt, for You are there,
Your rod and staff direct my way.

You spread my board before my foes,
With flowing cup have oiled my head.
Kindness and mercy follow me
    On every day I live
And in the Lord's House I shall dwell,
    To lengthen out my days.

Ferrar Fenton (1832–1911) was a business man, born in Lincolnshire. From humble beginnings, he rose to be financial adviser to De Beers Diamond Monopoly. In retirement, he was a prolific writer on linguistic and Biblical subjects, but his translation of the Bible (1904) has alone survived: he claimed that the work of translation took 50 years and was from the original tongues. His Bible became popular and went into several editions up to 1966.

I have a Shepherd, One I love so well,
How He has blessed me, tongue can never tell;
On the cross He suffered, shed His blood and died,
That I might ever in His love confide.

Chorus (after each verse)
Following Jesus, ever day by day,
Nothing can harm me when He leads the way;
Darkness or sunshine, whate'er befall,
Jesus, the Shepherd, is my All in All.

Pastures abundant doth His hand provide,
Still waters flowing ever at my side;
Goodness and mercy follow on my track,
With such a Shepherd nothing can I lack.

When I would wander from the path astray,
Then He will draw me back into the way;
In the darkest valley I need fear no ill,
For He, my Shepherd, will be with me still.

When labour's ended and the journey done,
Then He will lead me safely to my home;
There I shall dwell in rapture sure and sweet,
With all the loved ones gathered round His feet.

The Redemption Song Book *was first published in 1909 and is still in popular use. The author of the above version of the 23rd Psalm was Leonard Weaver, an evangelist of the early 1900s.*

THE LORD IS MY SHEPHERD

By Stopford Brooke

Beside still waters, where the grass
Is sweet and soft, by shadowy trees,
My Shepherd leads my weary feet
To give me ease.

This Shepherd is my Lord, my Love;
I shall not want; and when my soul
Is sick and heavy laden He
Restores it whole.

In paths of righteousness He guides
My erring steps, and if I go
Through the dark, shadowed vale of death
I find no foe.

For He is with me, and His staff
Guides me with love, and bids me take
Comfort and joy; and this He does
For His Name's sake.

When, in the hungry waste of life,
My heart is starved, He doth prepare
His wine and oil for my poor sprite,
And plenteous fare.

So, like a stream that sweetly runs
Beside my path, from lea to lea,
My Shepherd's goodness, year by year,
Has followed me.

And I shall dwell, when death shall bring
Me, wearied, to the eternal shore,
In His enclosed fold of peace
For evermore.

*Stopford Brooke (1832–1914) was a Church of England clergy-
man but left the Church as he could not accept miracles. He
became a fashionable lecturer on literary topics and a preacher in
independent chapels. He published books on Milton, Tennyson,
Browning and Early English literature.*

He wrote this hymn when he was about 80 years of age.

THE SHEPHERD-LORD

By Rev. Carey Bonner

Each morning breaks in glory,
   Each evening ends in song,
Since Christ, the Lord, hath led me
   My Shepherd, wise and strong:
His wisdom plans my pathway—
   His strength supplies all need—
For every day is His day
   And life is life indeed.

   For rest, for food, for shelter,
      His love does aye provide:
   Fresh pastures, quiet waters,
      Are mine while by His side;
   His grace, my soul restoring—
      Each day is found the same;
   In ways of right he leads me
      Because of His great Name.

The vale of death's dark shadow
   To me no ill can bring;
Thou, Shepherd-Lord, art with me,
   So—in the dark—I sing:
'Thy rod and staff, my comfort—
   Thy love my theme of praise—
Thy presence, my protection—
   Thyself, my King always.'

   'When evil foes surround me
      And threaten to molest—
   E'en then—in grace most wondrous—
      Thou makest me Thy guest:
   Thy goodness and Thy mercy
      Shall always follow me—
   And I will dwell for ever,
      O Shepherd-Lord, with Thee.'

Rev. Carey Bonner (1859–1938) gave this version in manuscript to Henry T. Uden (Hampstead) who thinks it was never published. Rev. Carey Bonner was a Baptist Minister and musician—

successively Minister of Union Chapel, Sale, and of Portland Chapel, Southampton. He became President of the Baptist Union of Great Britain and Ireland, the General Secretary of the National Sunday School Union, and Joint Secretary of World Sunday School Union. He wrote many hymns especially for children and compiled the Sunday School Hymnal. He also translated from the Bengali.

HE GUIDES ME

From the Moffatt Translation of the Bible

The Eternal shepherds me, I lack for nothing;
he makes me lie in meadows green,
he leads me to refreshing streams,
he revives life in me.

He guides me by true paths, as he himself is true.
My road may run through a glen of gloom,
but I fear no harm, for thou art beside me;
thy club, thy staff—they give me courage.

Thou art my host, spreading a feast for me,
while my foes have to look on!
Thou hast poured oil upon my head,
my cup is brimming over;
yes, and all through my life
Goodness and Kindness wait on me,
the Eternal's guest
within his household evermore.

The Reverend James Moffatt (1870–1944) was born in Glasgow and emigrated to the United States in 1927. An Independent Minister, he became Professor of Theology at the Union Theological Seminary in New York. He was a voluminous writer on theological subjects. His translation of the New Testament (1913) and of the Old Testament (1934) have become classics and are successful pioneer attempts to translate the Bible into the words of Everyman.

A PSALM.   DAVID'S

Yahweh is my Shepherd, I lack nothing;
he maketh me to lie down in green pastures,
Beside still waters doth he lead me,
he refresheth my soul;
He guideth me into paths of righteousness for his name's
    sake.
Yea, though I go through a valley of darkness,
I fear no evil,
With me is thy rod and thy staff,
they guide me.
Thou spreadest out a table before me,
in the presence of mine enemies;
Thou anointest my head with oil,
my cup overfloweth;
Yea, goodness and lovingkindness shall follow me
all the days of my life;
And I will dwell in the house of Yahweh
for length of days.

*This version by the Reverend W. O. E. Oesterley (1866–1950)
appeared in his book:* The Psalms, *published by SPCK in 1939.*

*W. O. E. Oesterley was a Prebendary of St Paul's Cathedral,
Professor of Hebrew and Old Testament Studies at King's College,
London, and Examiner in Hebrew at the Universities of Cambridge,
Durham, London, Bristol, Wales and Liverpool. He was the author
of a considerable number of books on Old Testament history,
theology and psychic research, and was a noted translator from
the Hebrew.*

In The Psalms *he added text-critical notes and a commentary
on each psalm. Commenting on Psalm 23 he said: 'The picture of*
Yahweh *as* Shepherd *is one in which the central thought is that
of his loving care for the helpless. It is used here in reference to
the individual psalmist, but elsewhere Yahweh is thought of as
the "Shepherd of Israel" . . . so that while in such passages as
these (other psalms quoted) it is the flock that he shepherds, here
he tends a single member of the flock. . . . It points to the growing
sense of the importance of the individual. . . .'*

THE VERSION OF MRS ALFRED MATHIESON

The Lord is my Shepherd, then why should I fear?
He'll feed me and guide me each day of the year;
In pastures so green and where still waters flow,
He'll lead me aright as with Him I go.

And if I should falter or faint on the track,
He restoreth my soul and bringeth me back;
In pathways of righteousness He leadeth me,
His rod and His staff my comfort shall be.

And if through the valley of shadow I go,
He still will be with me, He promised me so;
I need fear no evil with Him as my Guide,
For He will support me whatever betide.

His goodness and mercy will follow me still,
As together we walk over vale or uphill,
Until He shall lead me right up to His Throne,
The sheep of His flock, His loved and His own.

This version was one of many collected by the author's husband and published in his Everybody's Psalm *(1947).*

THE VERSION OF RONALD KNOX

The Lord is my Shepherd; how can I lack anything?

He gives me a resting-place where there is green pasture, leads me out to the cool water's brink, refreshed and content.

As in honour pledged, by sure paths he leads me; dark be the valley about my path, hurt I fear none while he is with me; thy rod, thy crook are my comfort. Envious my foes watch, while thou dost spread a banquet for me: richly thou dost anoint my head with oil, well filled my cup.

All my life thy loving favour pursues me; through the long years the Lord's house shall be my dwelling-place.

Ronald Knox (1888–1957) was received into the Roman Catholic Church in 1917. He became Catholic Chaplain of Oxford University. His books include detective stories, satires and theological works.

PSALM 23 IN BASIC ENGLISH BIBLE

The Lord takes care of me as his sheep: I will not be without any good thing. He makes a resting-place for me in the green fields, he is my guide by the quiet waters. He gives new life to my soul: he is my guide in the ways of righteousness because of his name. Yes, though I go through the valley of deep shade, I will have no fear of evil: for you are with me, your rod and your support are my comfort. You make ready a table for me in front of my haters: you put oil on my head; my cup is overflowing. Truly, blessing and mercy will be with me all the days of my life; and I will have a place in the house of the Lord all my days.

The Basic English New Testament was published in 1941, followed by the complete Bible twenty years later.

Basic English was developed by C. K. Ogden between 1926 and 1930 and was a courageous attempt to create an international auxiliary language. Reduced to 850 words (somewhat more for the translation of the Bible), Basic English allows of no synonyms to suggest differing shades of meaning and this resulted in some ambiguity. In E. F. Bruce's The English Bible. A History of Translations *(1961), the author states in chapter 13 that the capacity of Basic English to reproduce Biblical poetry is illustrated in the rendering of Psalm 23; and Sir Herbert Grierson in his study of Biblical translations wrote 'that it was not wanting in dignity'.*

PSALM 22 (23)

God, shepherd and host: A psalm of confidence

The Lord is my shepherd;
there is nothing I shall want.
Fresh and green are the pastures
where he gives me repose.
Near restful waters he leads me,
to revive my drooping spirit.

He guides me along the right path;
he is true to his name.
If I should walk in the valley of darkness
no evil would I fear.
You are there with your crook and your staff;
with these you give me comfort.

You have prepared a banquet for me
in the sight of my foes.
My head you have anointed with oil;
my cup is overflowing.

Surely goodness and kindness shall follow me
all the days of my life.
In the Lord's own house shall I dwell
for ever and ever.

The Psalms: A New Translation. *This translation from the Hebrew is the work of a team of scholars; it has been arranged for singing to the psalmody of Joseph Gelineau (1963).*

AN ENGLISH VERSION

By Frank Kendon

THE LORD is my shepherd: I shall want for nothing.
    He bids me lie down in green pastures;
He leads me along by the side of still waters,
    He renews life within me.
He guides me in paths that are right, for the name that he
        bears.
Even though I walk through a valley deep in darkness
    I fear no evil; for thou art with me;
Thy staff and thy cudgel in thy hand, these reassure me.

Thou dost set out a table ready before me
    In full sight of my enemies;
And hast lavished oil upon my head;
    My wine-cup is full and brimming over.
Only goodness, and love unfailing, shall follow me
    All the days of my life;
And in the Lord's house shall I make my home
    As long as I live.

Frank Kendon (1893–1959) was a poet of the Georgian move-
ment, a novelist and author of an autobiography : The Small
Years, *to which Walter de la Mare wrote an introduction.*
    His Thirty-Six Psalms *were published posthumously in 1963.*
He died while working on Old Testament translations for the
New English Bible.

FROM THE REVISED PSALTER: CONVOCATION OF CANTERBURY & YORK (1963)

The Lord is my Shepherd:
Therefore can I lack nothing.

He shall make me lie down in green pastures:
And lead me forth beside waters of comfort.

He shall refresh my soul:
And bring me forth in the right way for his names sake.

Yea, though I walk through the darkest valley, I will fear no
evil:
For thou art with me, thy rod and thy staff comfort me.

Thou shalt prepare a table before me, in the presence of
them that trouble me:
Thou hast anointed my head with oil and my cup shall be
full.

Yea, thy loving-kindness and mercy shall follow me all the
days of my life:
And I will dwell in the house of the Lord for ever.

The committee working on the Revised Psalter sat under the chairmanship of Dr Donald Coggan, then Archbishop of York, later of Canterbury. The terms of reference were: 'To produce for the consideration of Convocation a revision of the Psalter designed to remove obscurities and serious errors of translation, yet such as to retain . . . the general style and rhythm of Coverdale's version and its suitability for congregations.'

The Psalter was first published in 1961 and slightly revised for a 1963 edition. It retains much of the language of Coverdale.

PSALM 23 FROM THE JERUSALEM BIBLE

Yahweh is my shepherd,
I lack nothing.

In meadows of green grass he lets me lie.
To the waters of repose he leads me;
there he revives my soul.

He guides me by paths of virtue
for the sake of his name.

Though I pass through a gloomy valley,
I fear no harm;
beside me your rod and your staff
are there to hearten me.

You prepare a table before me
under the eyes of my enemies;
you anoint my head with oil,
my cup brims over.

Ah, how goodness and kindness pursue me,
every day of my life;
my home, the house of Yahweh,
as long as I live!

The French Bible de Jérusalem *was published in Paris 1950
and republished with the collaboration of Joseph Gelineau in 1955.
A sung or recited psalmody was composed on the basis of the
analogy between the Hebrew tonic rhythm and that of our
modern languages, English and French. In England* The Grail
*published an English translation based on the same principle as the
French; in 1956 the first collection of Psalms (24) appeared,
arranged for singing. In 1963 all of the 150 Psalms were
published in the Fontana edition.*

PSALM 23: FROM FIFTY PSALMS

An Attempt at a New Translation (1968)

My shepherd is the Lord,
I shall never want for anything.

He takes me to an oasis of green—
there I stretch out at the edge of the water,
where I find rest.
I come to life again, then we go forward
along trusted roads—he leads the way.
For God is his Name.

Although I must enter the darkness of death,
I am not anxious since you are with me—
In your keeping I dare to do it.

You invite me to sit at your table,
and all my enemies, with envious eyes,
have to look on while you wait upon me,
while you anoint me, my skin and my hair,
while you fill up my cup to the brim.

Happiness and mercy are coming to meet me
everywhere, every day of my life.
And always I go back to the house
of the Lord, as long as I live.

Fifty Psalms *is an attempt by Dutch and English scholars and poets to translate them into a new form which would be acceptable today and suitable in all kinds of situations. The original Dutch translation was published in 1967,· the English translation, with introduction and commentaries to each psalm, was published in 1968.*

PSALM 23 (22)

Psalm of confidence in Yahweh, as shepherd of the faithful (vv. 1–4) and as host at the meal associated with the thanksgiving sacrifice in the Temple (vv. 5–6)

The Lord is my shepherd   *Dominus me regit*

1   The Lord himself is my shepherd,
      What more could anyone ask!

2   In green meadows he pastures me,
      to quiet waters he leads me,
        there he restores my strength.

3   He guides me by paths of virtue
        for love of his name.

4   I fear nothing lurking
        in the dark ravine,
      with your weighted crook beside me
        to encourage me.

5   You prepare a banquet for me
        under my enemies' eyes;
      you perfume my head with oil
        and fill my cup.

6   Yes, goodness and kindness pursue me
        every day of my life;
      my home, the house of the Lord
        as long as I live!

After the Jerusalem Bible was published, a new version of the Psalms, based on the Jerusalem Bible and entitled The Jerusalem Bible—The Psalms for Reading and Recitation *was published. The editor was Alan Neame, one of the translators of the Jerusalem Bible. He said he aimed: 'to bring out the literary patterns inherent in the psalms: the symmetries, the antitheses, the devices, the refrains, the quotations, the liturgical dialogues'.*

PSALM 23.   FROM THE NEW ENGLISH BIBLE 1970

The Lord is my shepherd; I shall want nothing.
 He makes me lie down in green pastures,
and leads me beside the waters of peace;
 he renews life within me,
and for his name's sake guides me in the right path.
Even though I walk through a valley dark as death
I fear no evil, for thou art with me,
thy staff and thy crook are my comfort.

Thou spreadest a table for me in the sight of my enemies;
 thou hast richly bathed my head with oil,
 and my cup runs over.
Goodness and love unfailing, these will follow me
 all the days of my life,
 and I shall dwell in the house of the Lord
 my whole life long.

Work on the Old Testament occupied a group of scholars and literary advisers for twenty years; they aimed to make the translation as accurate and as intelligible to the modern reader as possible. It is not the expression of any denominational or doctrinal standpoint, but was undertaken by the major Christian bodies of the British Isles—other than the Roman Catholic Church which sent observers.

The translation was from the original Greek and Hebrew texts, and the translators aimed (in the words of the prospectus) at a version in current English 'founded on the resources of modern scholarship'. The New Testament was published in 1961, the Old Testament and the Apocrypha in 1970.

THE SHEPHERD PSALM IN THE LIVING BIBLE (1971)

Because the Lord is my Shepherd, I have everything I need!
He lets me rest in the meadow grass and leads me beside
the quiet streams.
He restores my failing health.
He helps me do what honors him the most.

Even when walking through the dark valley of death I will
not be afraid, for you are close beside me, guarding,
guiding all the way.

You provide delicious food for me in the presence of my
enemies.
You have welcomed me as your guest; blessings overflow!

Your goodness and unfailing kindness shall be with me all
of my life, and afterwards I will live with you forever
in your home.

The Living Bible *is an American paraphrase by Dr Kenneth
Taylor, first published in the United States in 1967 and in
Britain in 1971. It is particularly popular with young people
and the pop star, Cliff Richard, is reported to have said: 'It reads
like today's newspaper'.*

PSALM 23: HYMN 78 IN PSALM PRAISE

The Lord is my Shepherd, so nothing I lack,
He makes me in pastures to lie,
Beside the still waters He gently will lead,
My needs He will daily supply.

The Lord is my Saviour, my soul He restores,
He found me when lost and astray;
He shows me the way of His Truth and His Will
And helps me to trust and obey.

The Lord is my shield, I no evil shall fear,
He lightens the dark paths I tread;
He always is near me, with rod and with staff,
And now death itself has no dread.

The Lord is my strength, at His table I find
The power to defeat all my foes,
My life He sustains with His kindness and grace,
With blessing my cup overflows.

The Lord is my song, of His love I will sing,
I'll dwell in His house all my days;
His goodness and mercy will follow me still,
His Name I for ever will praise.

This version appeared in Psalm Praise *published by the Church Pastoral Aid Society in 1973. The book was sponsored by the Rev. Michael Baughen, Vicar of All Souls, Langham Place, London. The words of the version were written by Rev. J. E. Seddon of Peldon Rectory, Colchester, and they were set to music by Norman Warren. The writer has been a missionary in Morocco, and curate and vicar in Liverpool and Ipswich dioceses. He is interested in folk music and has written hymns in colloquial Arabic.*

The Lord is my shepherd:
therefore can I lack nothing.

He will make me lie down in green pastures:
and lead me beside still waters.

He will refresh my soul:
and guide me in right pathways for his name's sake.

Though I walk through the valley of the shadow
    of death, I will fear no evil:
for you are with me, your rod and your staff comfort me.

You spread a table before me in the face of those
    who trouble me:
you have anointed my head with oil, and my cup will be
    full.

Surely your goodness and loving-kindness
    will follow me all the days of my life:
and I shall dwell in the house of the Lord for ever.

    Glory to the Father, and to the Son,
        and to the Holy Spirit:
    as it was in the beginning, is now,
        and shall be for ever.   Amen.

This version is very close to Coverdale. It appears in the Series 3 Funeral Services and is one of the psalms in Twenty-five Psalms from a Modern Liturgical Psalter *by Dr D. L. Frost and Rev. A. A. Macintosh. Series 3 was presented to the General Synod of the Church of England in 1973 and was authorised for experimental use for a four-year period from June 1975.*

PSALM 23 THE LORD OUR SHEPHERD

The Lord is my Shepherd;
I have everything I need.
He lets me rest in fields of green grass
And leads me to quiet pools of fresh water,
He gives me new strength.
He guides me in the right paths as he promised.
Even if I go through the deepest darkness,
I will not be afraid, Lord,
For you are with me,
Your Shepherd's rod and staff protect me.

You prepare a banquet for me,
Where all my enemies can see me;
You welcome me as an honoured guest
And fill my cup to the brim.
I know that your goodness and love will be with me
    all my life
And your house will be my home
As long as I live.

The Good News Bible. *The New Testament was published in 1966 and the Old Testament in America in 1976. The complete Bible was first published in England in 1976 by the British and Foreign Bible Society and Messrs William Collins, with slight differences from the American text to conform with English usage.*

God is my shepherd, I shall not want.
He will bring me into meadows of young grass,
He will guide me beside quiet water.
He will strengthen my soul;
He will lead me in the path of justice, because of his name.
And when I walk in the valley of the darkness of death
I shall fear no evil, because you are with me,
Your crook and your staff will be my comfort.
You will set a table for me in front of my enemies;
You have anointed my head with oil, and my cup overflows.
Your goodness and mercy shall certainly follow me through
    all the days of my life,
And I shall live in the house of God for the length of my
    days.

This version is by Peter Levi, born 1931. He is a classical scholar, a poet and an archaeologist. He is at present (1977) a tutor in Classical Literature at Campion Hall, Oxford. His original poems have been published by Penguin and he has edited a Penguin Selection of the Poems of Alexander Pope.

Scottish and Shetlandic Versions

The Lord maist hie
I know will be
An herd to me;
I cannot lang have stress, nor stand in neid,
He makes my lair,
In field maist fair,
Quhair I bot care,
Reposing at my pleasure, safety feid.
He sweetly me convoys,
Quhair naething me annoys,
But pleasure brings.
He brings my mynd
Fit to sic kynd.
That foes, or fears of foe cannot me grieve.
He does me leid
In perfect freid,
And for His name He never will me lieve.
Thoch I wald stray,
Ilk day by day,
In deidly way.
Yet will I not dispair; I fear none ill,
For quhy Thy grace,
In every place,
Does me embrace,
Thy rod and shepherd's crook me comfort still.
In spite of foes
My tabil grows,
Thou balms my head with joy;
My cup overflows,
Kyndness and grace,
Mercy and peice,
Sall follow me for all my wretched days,
And me convoy,
To endless joy,
In heaven quhair I sall be with Thee always.

Alexander Montgomerie (c. 1556–1610) served James VI, and it is said that he turned all the Psalms into Scottish rhyme. He was appointed Poet Laureate to the Scottish court. He wrote Scottish verse of considerable charm.

THE TWENTY-THIRD PSALM

The Lord my scheepherd is, of want
I never shal complaine
for me to rest on hee doth grant
green pastures of the plaine.

Hee leads mee stillest streams beside
And doth my soul reclame
in righteous paths hee me doth guide
for glory of his name.

The valley dark of death's aboad
to passe, I'll fear no ill,
for thou art with me Lord; thy rod
and staffe me comfort still.

For me a table thou dost spread
in presence of my foes
with oyle thou dost anoint my head
by thee my cup overflows.

Mercie and goodness all my dayes
with me sall surelie stay
and in thy house, thy name to praise
Lord I will duell for ay.

This was written by Sir William Mure of Rowallan in 1629, and published in Rambles Round Kilmarnock, *by Archibald R. Adamson. Sir William Mure (1594–1657) Scottish poet and Royalist, fought at Marston Moor and commanded a regiment at Newcastle in 1644. He left numerous manuscripts of verse; much of it was published posthumously.*

Wha is my shepherd weel I ken
The Lord himself is He
He leads me whaur the girse is green
An' burnies quate that be.

Aft times I fain astray wad gang
An' wann'r far astray
He fin's me oot, He pits me richt
An' brings me hame an' a'.

Though I pass through the gruesome cleugh
Fin' I ken He is near
His muckle crook will me defend
Sae I hev nought tae fear.

Ilk comfort that a sheep could need
His thoughtful care provides
Though wolves and dogs may prowl aboot
In safety He me hides.

His goodness and His mercy baith
Nae doot will bide wi' me
While folded in the hills of time
For a' eternity.

Of the numerous Scottish versions of Psalm 23 collected by the Anthologists, the above would seem to be the best-loved for it has been sent in by several people. It was printed as recently as July 1975 in The Scots Magazine: *Mrs M. V. Watt of Edmonton, Alberta, sent it, saying she had seen it in* The Family Herald and Weekly Star. *It was written by John Moir, a blind poet of Banchory, Scotland, in the early eighteenth century.*

PSALM XXIII

Ane Psalm o' David

The Lord is my shepherd; I sallna inlak.

He mak's me til lye doun in green an' baittle gangs; he leeds me aside the quæet waters.

He refreschens my saul; he leeds me in the peths o' richteousniss for his næme's sak'.

Yis, thouch I wauk throwe the vallie o' the skaddaw o'deæth, I wull feær nae ill: for thou art wi' me; thy cruik an' thy staffe thaye comfirt me.

Thou prepairist me ane tabel in the preesince o' mine enimies: thou anaintist my heæd wi' oolie; my cupp rins ower.

Shurelie guidniss an' mercie sall follo me a' the dayes o my liffe; and I wull dwall in the hous o' the Lord forevir.

This is a Lowland Scots Version by Henry Scott Riddell (1798–1870). He was a minor Scottish poet, son of a shepherd. From 1831 he was Minister at Teviothead. He wrote the above version in 1857. He was a friend of Hogg, the Ettrick Shepherd. His 1857 versions of Psalms were written for Prince Lucien Bonaparte's collection of dialect versions of the Bible.

TWENTY-THIRD PSALM

The Lord to me's a Herd indeed,
I canna want for ony gweed;
He mak's me lie on reif o' green,
Whaur peacefu' waters aye are seen.

He purifies my soul frae sin,
Sets me upon my feet to rin
On the richt road, He dis it flake
To keep me safe for His Name's sake.

I winna fear when He is near,
Tho' death and darkness roun' me veer;
The darkest nicht wi' Him is clear
His rod will guide, His staff will cheer.

Tho' I'm wi' enemies set roun'
He loads my table up and doun
My heid wi' oil He dis weel weet,
My cup's aye runnin' over's ye seet

He's gweed an' mercifu' to me,
Thro' life I ne'er doot but He'll be.
Sine in His ain house He'll keep me
For time and for eternity.

This version was composed by Thomas Gill, and was published in his Thoughts Unspoken *in 1897.*

TWENTY-THIRD PSALM

The Lord my guide has been;
  No want my soul shall know,
He leadeth me through pastures green,
  Where living waters flow.

The verdant plains are fair,
  The waters calm and sweet;
O how I love to linger there,
  Where all my blessings meet.

In bless'd content we sit
  But only rest a day—
'Tis but a breathing space to fit
  Us for the rougher way.

Protecting care I know
  Each morning as I wake,
He'll keep me all the way below,
  Even for His own name's sake.

Upon a barren track
  My footsteps went astray;
His loving kindness brought me back
  Into the narrow way.

Though down into the vale
  Of shadows I descend,
They shall not find their strength to fail
  Who on his love depend.

For in this gloomy land
  His presence I shall see,
And feel the pressure of His hand
  So gently leading me.

And so in perfect peace,
  No evil I shall fear;
His promises shall never cease
  In comforting me here.

His blessed rod and staff
  Shall be my strength and stay.
His purposes on my behalf
  Are ripening every day.

And even here below
　Mine enemies shall see,
How in His kind and gracious way,
　The Lord has honoured me.

With blessings from His word
　My cup is running o'er;
And in the presence of the Lord
　I'll dwell for evermore.

This version, by William Tulloch, a Shetlander, folllows in the Scottish tradition of metrical settings. William Tulloch was born in the island of Fetlar in 1870; he went as a young man to Lerwick where he was a general merchant for the rest of his life. A member of a god-fearing family, he wrote a number of poems and contributed to The Shetland News, *under the pen-name of* ANOF (*A Native Of Fetlar*).

TWENTY-THIRD PSALM IN BRAID SCOTS

The Lord o' Heaven my Shepherd is,
    He will me ever lead:
Will every want o' mine supply,
    Nor stint my daily breid.

In bonny howes wi' pastures green
    He'll mak' me lie amang;
Or by the wimplin' burnie clear
    He'll lead me a' day lang.

And when I've wandered frae His fold
    He brocht me back again;
And led me on when apt tae fa'
    On ilka slippery stane.

When death wi' his cauld grasp shall come—
    What ha'e I then to fear?
For through the valley's mirk and gloom
    His rod and staff will cheer.

A table he has denty set
    Mine enemies before;
My head is streakit doon wi' oil;
    My cup is runnin' owre.

Guidness and mercy suirely shall
    Gang wi' me a' my days;
Until I reach His hame abune,
    And sing for aye His praise.

A. R. Paton published a book of poems: Stray Leaves *in 1900 and the above version of Psalm 23 'in braid Scots' appeared in the book.*

TWENTY-THIRD PSALM

(Dauid is aye unreelin' a pirn aboot Christ. Here he pents him as a Shepherd and his sel as a silly bit lammie. It evens weel wi' the tenth o' John.)

The Lord is my shepherd; my wants are a' kent; the pasture I lie on is growthie and green.

    I follow by the lip o' the waters o' Peace.

    He heals and sterklie hauds my saul; and airts me for his ain names sake, in a' the fit roads o' his holiness.

    Aye, and though I bude gang throwe the howe whaur the died shadows fa', I'se fear nae skaith nor ill. For that yersel is aye aside me; yere rod and yere cruik they aye defend me.

    My table ye hae plenish't afore the een o' my foes; my heid ye hae cheeptit wi' yle; my cup is teemin' fu'.

    And certes, tenderness and mercie sal be my fa' to the end o' my days; and syne I'se bide i' the hoose o' the Lord, for evir and evir mair.

This version was composed by Rev. William Wye Smith and appeared in his New Testament in Braid Scots, *published in Paisley in 1904. His reference in the sub-title of the psalm to 'tenth o' John' is a reminder that the Gospel of John, chapter 10, contains our Lord's parables about the shepherd and his sheep.*

THE TWENTY-THIRD PSALM

The Lord is my herd, nae want sal fa me,
He louts me till lie amang green howes.
He airts me atower be the lown watters.
He waukens ma wa-gaen saul, He weises me roon for His
    ain name's sake until right roddans.
Na, though I gang through the deid mirk dail, e'en thar sal
    I dreed nae skaithin, for yersel' are narby me, yer stock
    and yer stay haud me baith fu' cheerie.
Ma baird ye hae hanselled in the face o' my faes. Ye hae
    drookit ma heid wi' ail, ma bicker is fu' and skailin'.
Een sae sal guid guidin' and guid gre gang wi' me ilk day
    o' ma leevin, and wer mair syne i' the Lord's ain hows
    at lang last sal I mak bydan.

*This version was sent by George F. Stirling of Victoria, British
Columbia; it was taught him by his grandmother who lived in
Southern Scotland in the nineteenth century and he thought it was
old in her time. Some of the words—for example 'ma wa-gaen
saul' and 'roddans'—are to be found in 'Psaum 23' on page 100.*

PSALM 23 IN SHETLANDIC

Da Lord is my awner
  Nae want sall I ken;
He bules me a sinner
  In fields growin' green.

He leds me by shores
  Whaur waters ir still,
My sowl He restores:
  And keeps me fae ill.

Fur da sake o' His Name,
  Yea, though I sud tread
Troo death's mirk gaun hame,
  Nae evil I'll dreed.

Fur Thou wilt be wi' me
  Dy rod an' Dy staff,
Dey comfirt sall gie me,
  An keep trouble aff.

Thou my table haes spread
  Whaur enemies rage;
Wi oil dressed my head;
  My cup's ower the adge.

Sae His love 'ill never
  In my lifetime fail;
In God's hoose forever
  I'll bide wi Himsel'.

*This was sent by Kate Moar, a Shetlander of Yell, Shetland;
she said it was written by James Hunter (1872–1920) born at
Billister, Nesting, Shetland.*

TWENTY-THIRD PSALM

E'en as a shepherd tents his sheep,
　　The Lord for me doth fend,
He mak'st me rest, whaur pasture's best,
　　And wimplin' waters wend.

Sood my soul ail, He mak's it hale
　　And airts my feet to gang
For his name's sake, the bonny gait,
　　Whaur's nocht o' ill or wrang.

When I am boon to travel doon
　　The mirkey Glen o' Daith,
Nae dreid I bruik, His staff and crook,
　　Sal haud me free o' skaith.

Wi' ample fare, Thou dost prepare
　　My board, while faemen glow'r,
Wi' ointment fine my heid dis shine,
　　My bicker's skailing ower.

Guidness and mercy a' my days,
　　Are siccar at my side:
And in God's name, I'll be fu' fain
　　For evermair to bide.

This version was composed by the Rev. T. T. Alexander, Minister
of St Ninian's U.F. Church, Leith, sometime in the 1920s.

JOHN A. ANDERSON'S VERSION

The Laird's My Herd

The Laird's my Herd, I sall nae want,
  He loots me to lie doon,
Atowre the knowes, an' in green howes,
  Whaur bonnie burnies croon.

My soul He waukins frae its dwaum,
  Out o' the muirland weet,
Intil richt roads—for His name's sake—
  He airts my wann'ring feet.

Na, tho' I hae to gang my lane,
  Doon through the deid mirk dale,
I'll thole nae skaith, for Ye are bye,
  Yer crook an' kent ne'er fail.

My grainin' buird Ye've hansellt, while
  My faes did sit an' glower,
My pow wi' ile is dreepin' wat,
  My bicker's lippin' ower.

Guid guidin' an guid greein' sail
  Gang wi' me late an' air,
An' syne up i' the Laird's big hoose
  I'll bide for ever mair.

This version is one of many sent to The Scots Magazine. *It was sent by Mr Frank Wilson of Eldwick, Yorkshire, who had found it in a book* The Cleikum *written by John A. Anderson, who died in 1932 at Harrow.*

94

THE TWENTY-THIRD PSALM

The Lord's my herd, at every turn,
    He gie's me a' I need:
He leads me doon beside the burn
    And through the grassy mead.

And whiles, when I hae lost the track
    And some wrang turnings take,
His tender mercy brings me back,
    E'en for His ain name's sake.

Aye! tho' He leads me thro' the land,
    Where daith's dread shadows be;
I'll tak' His staff into my hand
    And that's eneuch for me.

'Mang freends an foes, I aye hae meat
    Wi' kindness never failin';
He gies me mair than I can eat,
    My bicker's fu' and skailin'.

Guidness, I trow, will follow me
    And mercy leave me never;
Till I wi' Thee, a dweller be
    For ever and for ever.

This version was seen in a newspaper by Miss Campbell of Largs, Ayrshire; the date of the newspaper is probably about 1940 but the date of the version is not given, nor the name of the author.

PSALM 23 IN VERSE

The Lord is my Shepherd, in nocht am I wantin',
In the haughs o' green girse does He mak me lie doon,
While mony puir straiglers are bleatin' and pantin',
By saft flowing burnies He leads me at noon.

When since I had strayed far awa' in the bracken,
And daidled till gloaming cam' ower a' the hills,
Nae dribble o' water my sair drooth to slacken,
And dark growed the nicht wi' its harrs and its chills.

Awa frae the fauld, strayin' fit-sair and weary,
I thocht I had naethin' to dea but to dee,
HE socht me and fand me in mountain hechts dreary,
HE gangs by fell paths which HE kens best for me.

And noo for HIS names sake, I'm dune wi a' fearing,
Though cloods may aft gaither and soughin' winds blaw,
'Hoo this' or 'Hoo that'—oh, prevent me frae speirin',
HIS wull is aye best, and I daurna say na'.

The valley of death winna fleg me to thread it,
Though awfu' darkness, I weel can foresee,
Wi HIS rod and HIS Staff HE wull help me to tread it,
And then wull its shadows, sae gruesome, all flee.

For fochin, in presence o' foes that surround me,
MY SHEPHERD a table wi denties has spread,
The thyme and the myrtle blow fragrant aroond me,
HE brims a fu' cup and poors oil on my head.

Surely goodness and mercy despite a' my roamin'
Wull gang wi me doon to the brink o' the river,
Ayont it nae mair o' the eerie and gloaming,
I wull bide in the HAME o' my FAITHER for ever.

This version, which was published in The Weekly Scotsman, *is
said to have been recited by an old farm labourer in Midlothian
some time this century.*

PSALM 23

The Lord is my herd, sae nocht shall I lack, He gaulds me i' the bughts by the haughs sae green, He gars me farrit by the lechans lown whaur He slockens my sould.

He wiseth me the road that's richt for me to tak'. Aye, gin my gart's i' the mirk o' the glen o' the gloam o' deid, I shall fear fient a haet, for Thou art wi' me. Thy rung and Thy crummock, they fend for me.

Thou penishest my board i' the face o' me faes, Thou anointest my brow wi' the oil o' the unction o' Thy grace. My coggie's lippin' fu'.

Siccarly, I trow Thy bounty will aye be ahint me or I win awa' and at the hinner end I shall bide but and ben wi' the Lord, aye and for aye.

This version was one of those published in The Weekly Scotsman; *it was written by Rev. James L. Dow of Greenock—who died in 1977.*

THE KILKERRAN SHEPHERD: PSALM XXIII

Wha but the Lord will be my herd?
By Girvan Water's side he's led me,
And in the bonnie holms of Aird
With heavenly pasture he has fed me.

My feckless soul he'll turn and bless,
E'en through the glamour of his name,
Intae the pads o' righteousness,
Sweeter nor a' the roads o' hame.

Though in Death's glowerin' glen I gang,
Nae scunner will it gar me gie,
Thou'rt at my side, thy kent is lang,
And surely it will comfort me.

A table for me thou hast spreid,
Where nane can win wad wark my doom,
Thy clouds drop fatness on my heid,
My tass has never fallen toom.

Thy kindliness will follow me,
Fu' well I ken it—a' my days,
And I will bigg a house to thee,
Where'er I gang, o' prayer and praise.

This version was published in Lowland Soldier *by Bernard Fergusson, 1945.*

PSAUM 23 IN LALLANS

The Lord is my herd; he kens aa my wants.
He gars me ligg i' the growthie leys
An' leads me by the lip o the lown watir.
For his ain name's sake he maks me hale
An' airts me i' the richt gate.
Albeid I gang thru' the howe o the scaddows o daith
I'll fear nae skaith;
For Yersel is my feir
An' yer rod an' cruik sal bield me.
My buird ye hae plenish't afore the een o my faes
An' my heid ye hae chrystit wi' oyle;
My tassie's lippin-fu'.
Certes, aa that's guid, aa that's merciefu', sal aye be my fa',
An' I'll bide i' God's kirk for evir an' evir mair.

F. J. Nicholson, born 1903, is a member of the Society of Friends, and is a graduate (M.A.) of Edinburgh University. He is a writer and poet and a member of the Lallans Society. His version of Psalm 23 appeared in The Friend *in May 1973.*

PSAUM 23 TRANSLATED INTIL SCOTS

The Lord's ma herd, I sall want nocht
He gars me doun tae ligg
Amang howes haw by wattirs lown
Ma wabbit saul tae bigg

Ma wa-gaen saul He waukens up
In roddins richt tae spail
Frae ferture fell He weisit me
His bandoune wyce tae wale

Gin, I gae throu the died mirk dail
Nae ill can dae me skaith
Ye're nar me an yer rod and cruik
Ma beild an aird are baith

Ma tabyll Ye hae hanselt weel
Ye've cuisten doun ma faes
Ma heid wi oyle Ye've droukit aa
Ma bicker's fu aaways

Guidness an sainin aa ma life
Sall shairly bide wi me
Syne in God's hows for evirmair
I sall abidin be.

This translation 'intil Scots' was made by Rev. A. S. Borrowman and was first sung during the Annual Conference of the Lallans Society as part of the Kirk Service. Rev. A. S. Borrowman is minister at Glasgow St Andrew's Parish Kirk.

The Lallans Society uses 'Scotscrieve' and 'Scotsoun' to maintain the spelling and sound of the language. A translation into 'English' is given in the margin of the above version; perhaps it is sufficient here to say that ma wa-gaen saul *means* my errant soul, *and* roddins *mean* sheepwalks *and* spail *means* walk briskly.

A SHETLANDIC VERSION OF PSALM 23

Da Lord's my hird, I sanna want,
He finns me büls ithin
Green mudow girse, and leds me whaar
Da burns sae saftly rin.

He lukks my wilt and wanless sowl
Stravaigan far fae hame
Back tae da nairoo winding gait
For sake o His ain name.

Though I sood geng doon Daeth's dark gyill,
Nae ill sall come my wye,
For He will gaird me wi His staff,
An comfort me forbye.

My table He has coosed wi maet,
Whin fantin gödda fremd,
My cup wi hansels lippers ower,
My head wi oil is sained.

Noo shurly a my livin days
Gud's Love sall hap me ower,
An I sall win tae his ain hoose
Tae bide for evermore.

This version was given to a missioner of the Church of Scotland in Tingwall, Shetland, early in the twentieth century, but it dates back earlier than that.

THE 23RD PSALM O KING DAUVIT (FRAE THE HEBREW)

The Lord's my herd, I sall nocht want.
  Whaur green the gresses grow
sall be my fauld. He caas me aye
  whaur fresh sweet burnies rowe.

He gars my saul be blyth aince mair
  that wandert was frae hame,
and leads me on the straucht smaa gait
  for sake of His ain name.

Tho I suld gang the glen o mirk
  I'ld grue for nae mischance,
Thou bydes wi me, Thy kent and cruik
  maks aye my sustenance.

Thou spreids ane brod and gies me meat
  whaur aa my faes may view,
Thou sains my heid wi ulyie owre
  and pours my cogie fou.

Nou seil and kindliness sall gae
  throu aa my days wi me,
and I sall wone in God's ain hous
  at hame eternallie.

Douglas Young (1913–1973) was a Scottish classical scholar, poet and historian. He published a book of poems in 1947: A Braird o Thristles, and his version of Psalm 23 appeared in this book. It was sung at his memorial service in the University Chapel of St Andrews in January 1974.

Douglas Young was on the staff of St Andrews University before taking up an appointment at McMaster University, Ontario in 1968; he became Professor of Greek in the University of North Carolina where he died.

Pidgin and Dialect Versions

SAM 23 IN PIDGIN ENGLISH

Yawe i wasman bilong jumi

1   Mi olsem sipsip na Yawe i wasman bilong mi.
     Olsem na mi no inap sot long wanpela samting.

2   Em i mekim mi slip long gutpela gras.
     Em i bringim mi i go long ol wara bai mi dring na
       mi malolo.

3   Em i mekim orait spirit bilong mi gen.
     Em i save bringim mi long ol gutpela rot,
       olsem na mi litimapim nem bilong em.

4   Sapos mi wokabaut long ples nogut na bikpela tudak,
     maski mi no ken pret long samting nogut.
    Long wanem: Yu stap wantaim mi.
    Mi lukim yu holim stik bilong wasman na kanda bilong
      paitim wel abus,
     olsen na mi bel isi.

5   Yu redim gutpela kaikai bilong mi, na ol birua bilong
      mi ol i lukim.
    Yu kisim mi i kam sindaun wantaim yu,
      na yu lukautim mi gutpela tumas.

6   Yawe bai yu lukautim mi gut
      na yu marimari long mi olgeta yia mi stap laip.
    Na bai mi stap oltaim oltaim long haus bilong yu.

(Devit i raitim dispela sam.)

This Pidgin English version was sent by Mrs E. Dingle of Graceville, Australia, after her visit, on behalf of the Australasian Federation of Methodist Women, to New Guinea in February 1974. The Prince of Wales who was described in New Guinea as 'Misis Kwin nambawan pikinini' learned enough of the Pidgin English language to address a meeting of New Guineans in Pidgin, their native tongue.

PSALM 23 PUT INTO DE SUSSEX DIALECT

By James Richards of Tunbridge Wells

De Lord my Shepherd be
Surelye I shall not lack.
He leads me into fresh green grass
Along de daily track.
And where de waters sweet
Flow gently, gently on
He leads me; and He maaks me feel
dat I be He's own son.
My soul He does restore
and in right paths does guide
for He's naame's sake; and so dat I
doant wander from He's side.
Yea, though I walk tween hills
de shaades of death all through,
of evil I wunt be afeardt
acos I walk wid you.
Your kind of Sussex bat,
your kind of Pyecombe crook,
they comfort me: and 'sure me I
to you for help can look.
A table you've prepared
dere I may set and feast
where enemies be all around,
You'll see dey doant molest.
You've poured iol on my head
as ef I was a king;
my cup of jy runs over loike
a ever bubbling spring.
Goodness and marcy too
shall surelye follow me
all through de days of earthly life
wherever I may be.
   And surelye after dat
   in de house of de Lord
   I'll live for ever.
   For dat be according to He's word.

James Richards (1866–1949), son of a farmworker at Hailsham, Sussex, came to Tunbridge Wells where he had a newsagents shop. He became a lay preacher and put some books of the Bible into the old Sussex dialect which he loved. He printed them on his own 'liddle' press in Tunbridge Wells. He wrote: 'I am not an educated man, and can only approach dialect from the memory point of view; but I feel strongly that there is much more in dialects than most people think, more of the real language of the people than they imagine.'

He signed his published writings 'Jim Cladpole' and wrote doggerel verse as well as a humorous pamphlet about Tunbridge Wells and neighbourhood. A cyclist, he knew Tunbridge Wells thoroughly and set himself the task of taking photographs of all churches within his cycling radius.

The Master's me looker: so's I wants naun:
   He makes I fur to lay down in de green field:
     he goos lang wid me by de dewpans.
       He keeps me peert.
   He goos lang wid me on de hill for his goodness.

Ebm if I walks through de shadder in de bottom,
lookee, I arnt afeard:
   for thou'rt wid me; thy crook and thy bat comforts me.
   Thou gives me gryst afore them as goos agin me:
   thou bastes me head with iol and fobs me pot.

Worth and marcy'll foller I all me time, surelye,
   en I shall bide in Master's plaace evermore.

The author, W. G. Daish, lived at Wateringbury, Kent, and was on the staff of Whitbread's, Maidstone. He was really a Sussex man (educated at Christ's Hospital) and he loved and studied the Sussex dialect. He died in 1963.

A SHEPHERD'S VERSION

Thur Lord is me Shepherd, I sharn't want fur nothin'.

He goes afore me over thur green dowans, an guides me
by thur quiet waters o' thur Adur.

He comforts me soul, an leads me along good paaths
for His naame's sake.

Yea, though I walks thru thur shadowery ways I aunt
afeared, for His shepherd's crook'll guide me.

He'll fin' a quiet plaace fer to eat ower food
arter we overcome ower difficulties an' us'll be happy.

Shurlye this loveliness 'ul be wi' me aul me days
till I coome to thur hoome o' me Lord for ever.

The Countryman *magazine, Winter 1971/72: 'In June 1946
an old shepherd recited this to me, surrounded by his flock, on the
Downs above Steyning in Sussex.'—Kathleen Lee.*

A SCOUSE PARAPHRASE OF PSALM 23

I call Him me Shipmate, me butty. Tho a course e made me.
E won't see me stuck. E takes me away fum dicey joints into
gear placis. It's like avin a quiet walk along the Mersey
above Runcorn.

When I feel proper umpty E makes me feel gear. Jus so
I do credit to im e moodeys along wit me into the real
best specs in dis world. Ay, if I wuz on the way to the
bone-yard I'd not be scurred—dere e is—ay, you're durr,
mate, you gorra walkin' can AN a crutch to elp your ould
butty, la. Dem as ates yew, dey see me sittin down to good
scoff, you get me all poshed up and toney, I just can't say
ta enough. No argin about it, s'long as I live the gear tings
an' the elpin and'll be durr. An' in the nex werld.

*This was written by Frank Shaw, author (with Rev. Dick Williams)
of* Gospels in Scouse *(1968), and other books in the Liverpool
(scouse) dialect. He died in the early 1970s, and was writing in
scouse up to his final illness.*

PSALM 23 IN WENSLEYDALE DIALECT

The Lord is m' shipperd; Ah'll want fer nowt. He lets m' bassock i't' best pasters, an' taks m' bit' watter side whar o's wyat an peaceful. He uplifts mi soel an' maks things seea easy 'at Ah can dew whats reet an' gloryfy His neeam.

Evan if Ah cu't' Deeaths deursteead ahs nut bi freetend; fer He'll bi wi' me, His creuk an' esh plant 'll upho'd me. Thu puts a good meeal afoor me, reet anenst them 'at upbraids me.

Thu ceuls mi heead wi' oil an' Ah've meeat an' drink t' spar'. Seurlie Thi goodniss an' mercy 'al bi mine fer o't' day o' mi life, an Ah'll beleng t' t' hoose o' the Lord fer ivver.

Notes: Bassock   relax in leisurely contentment
       Anenst   against
       Upbraids challenges with lies

Paraphrase by Mr Kit Calvert who lives at Hawes, Yorkshire. He has been a dairyman all his working life; he is keenly interested in the Wensleydale dialect and has written part of the Gospels in this dialect. Now that he has retired he has found time to sell books.

PSALM 23 IN YORKSHIRE DIALECT

T'owd Boss luks after mi; ah want for nowt.
'e sees as 'ow there's fields weer ah c'n sit
    missen dahn,
or tek a walk alongside o' t' dams.

Bigod, ah feels missen agen.
's reight, t' foller 'im, 'cos e's t'Boss.

Aye, tho' t' valley's thick wi' smooak,
    an' Death's in it, ah'll fear nowt,
for th'art wi' mi, th'art mi backbooan an' mi
    walking-stick; tha keeps mi snug.

Tha ses: Sit thi dahn an' eeat;
    ne'er mind as theer's them as grudge thee it.

Tha smooths mi 'air, an' fills brimful mi mug.

F'shooa thi blessin' 'n compassion
    'll be wi' mi till smooak clears
    an' ah'm wi' thee
    in t'ouse that's allus, allus thine.

Anonymous Yorkshire version, Sheffield, 1922.

Modern Paraphrases

THE PILOT'S PSALM

The Lord is my Pilot, I shall not drift.

He lighteth me across the dark waters;
He steereth me in deep channels; He keepeth
my log. He guideth me by the Star of Holiness
for His Name's sake.

Yea, though I sail mid the thunders and tempests
of life, I will dread no danger, for Thou art
with me; Thy love and Thy care they shelter me.

Thou preparest a harbour before me in the homeland
of Eternity. Thou anointest the waves with oil.
My ship rideth calmly.

Surely sunlight and starlight shall favour me
on the voyage I take, and I will rest in the port
of my God for ever.

This version of the Twenty-third Psalm was written by a Captain John Roberts in 1874 and placarded on the wall of the Seamen's Institute by the harbour in Newlyn, Cornwall. Captain Booker, Retd., was a young seaman on the bark Inverurie *which rounded Cape Horn in 1906, and he remembers the Pilot's Psalm being used at the burial at sea of the* Inverurie's *carpenter.*

Captain Edward Downing, a lay-preacher of Mousehole, recorded it for a broadcast in the edition of Leslie Baily's Log Book, entitled: 'A Nice Bit of Fish'.

The Pilot's Psalm is displayed in various harbours, including that of Bridlington.

111

A TRANSLATION OF THE JAPANESE VERSION

The Lord is my Pace-setter, I shall not rush;
He makes me stop and rest for quiet intervals.

He provides me with images of stillness, which restore my
serenity;
He leads me in ways of efficiency through calmness of mind,
And His guidance is peace.

Even though I have a great many things to accomplish each
day,
I will not fret, for His presence is here.

His timelessness, His all importance, will keep me in
balance.

He prepares refreshment and renewal in the midst of my
activity
By anointing my mind with His oils of tranquillity.

My cup of joyous energy overflows.

Surely harmony and effectiveness shall be the fruits of my
hours,
For I shall walk in the peace of my Lord, and dwell in His
house for ever.

*This was broadcast by Rev. Eric Frost on 4th May 1965, from
London. It was composed by Toki Miyashina, a Japanese woman.*

THE 23RD PSALM, AS TRANSLATED BY AN AMERICAN INDIAN

The Great Spirit above is a Shepherd Chief, I am His, and with Him I want not.

He throws to me a rope, and the name of the rope is Love; and He draws me very tenderly to where the grass is green, and the water not dangerous, and I eat and lie down satisfied.

Sometimes my heart is very weak and falls down; but He lifts it up again, and draws me into a good road, for His name is Wonderful.

Sometime, it may be very soon, it may be longer, it may be a long, long time, He will draw me into a narrow place between mountains. It is dark there but I'll not turn back, and I'll not be afraid, for it is in there between those mountains that the Shepherd Chief will meet me, and the hunger I have felt in my heart all through this life will be satisfied.

Sometimes He makes the love rope into a whip, but afterwards He gives me a staff to lean on.

He spreads a table before me with all kinds of food, He puts His hand upon my head, and all the tiredness is gone.

He fills my cup till it runs over. What I tell you is true, it is no lie.

These roads that are away ahead will stay with me through this life, and afterwards I shall go to live in the big camp, and sit down with the Shepherd Chief for ever.

This appeared in Christ and the Fine Arts, *by Cynthia Pearl Maus, 1938.*

113

A MOUNTAINEER'S VERSION

By Christopher Johnson

My Guide is the Lord: he will not let me wander.
Through the deep rivers he holds firm my feet.
Up steep rock ridges his route will never falter.
He gives me courage in my time of need.
 For all my journey, his Book is my route guide.

Life's storms and thunder hold no fear with him.
His holding hands give strength and consolation.
In weather's worst, his hut will take me in.

 There will he treat my bruises, ease my stiffness,
His cup will comfort, and his food content.
Surely his guidance and his guard shall take me
Safe through my climbing days till Journey's End.

This was written in 1953, the year that the top of Mount Everest was first reached. Christopher Johnson lost his life on a mountain in New Zealand while searching for a missing climber. He is the subject of a chapter in Men Aspiring, *a book about mountaineers by Paul Powell of Dunedin, New Zealand.*

THE LORD IS LIKE MY PROBATION OFFICER—
PSALM 23

The Lord is like my Probation Officer,
  He will help me,
    He tries to help me make it every day.
    He makes me play it cool
      And feel good inside of me.
      He shows me the right path
        So I'll have a good record,
        And he'll have one too.

Because I trust him
  And that ain't easy,
    I don't worry too much about
      What's going to happen.
      Just knowing he cares about
      Me helps me.

He makes sure I have my food
  And that Mom fixes it.
    He helps her stay sober
      And that makes me feel good
      All over.

He's a good man, I think,
  And he is kind;
    And these things will stay
    With me.

And when I'm kind and good
  Then I know the Lord
    Is with me like the Probation Officer.

This version appears in God is for Real, Man *which was first published by YMCA, New York, in 1966; it was first published in Great Britain in 1967. Carl Burke is a chaplain in Erie County Jail, New York. Instead of trying to force the scriptures on the young men 'inside' he encourages them to retell the Bible stories in their own 'hip' language, the only rule being that they must keep the basic meaning.*

A TWENTY-THIRD PSALM FOR THE SPACE AGE

The Lord is my Controller, I shall not deviate;
He places me in true orbit around my planet Earth.
He plotteth my course across the vacuum of Space,
He directs me safely through the maze of Stars.
He guards my ship from the blazing meteorite,
He guides me securely to my purposed destination.
   Yea, though I move in the inter-stellar regions of Thy
      universe
   I will fear no perpetual Darkness nor heat of Sun;
   For thy Presence in the galaxies reassures me,
   Thy nearness in the heavens, it comforts me.
Lo! My space-craft is ever before Thine eyes,
And my 'touch-down' on landing, Thou preparedst long
      before.
   My outward and my homeward paths through Space
   Are thy Eternal habitations . . .
Therefore my voyage shall be along familiar ways,
And I will journey in the safe keeping of Thy love for ever.

This appeared in the Worcester Evening News *in May 1971
after Rev. Eric Hayman, curate of St John-in-Bedwardine,
Worcester, who wrote it, had read it to young people in a church
Family Service. Rev. Eric Hayman is now Vicar of Wrabness,
Manningtree.*

Acknowledgements

We thank the following for their help in providing versions and information, and also those who have given us permission to use copyright material.

The American Bible Society
Miss Gladys Anson
The Earl of Ballantrae (Bernard Fergusson)
Messrs A. & C. Black
The Rev. A. S. Borrowman
The Rev. J. C. Bowmer (of Methodist Archives)
The British and Foreign Bible Society
The British Library
The Rev. Carl Burke
Messrs Burns & Oates
The Cambridge University Press
Church Pastoral Aid
Miss G. E. Coldham, Librarian, British and
    Foreign Bible Society
Messrs William Collins
Messrs Darton, Longman & Todd and Doubleday & Co. Inc.
Mrs E. Dingle, Brisbane
Messrs Eyre & Spottiswoode
The Editor, 'The Friend'
The Governors of St Olave's and St Saviour's
    School
Mrs H. J. Grimshaw
Messrs Harper & Row
The Earl of Harrowby
The Rev. Eric Hayman
Professor A. D. Herbert
Messrs Hodder & Stoughton
Mr T. B. Honeyman, Mr Alex Thain and colleagues
    of The Saint Andrew Press
Hymns Ancient and Modern
John Johnson's Agency
Mrs E. C. P. Kendon
Kingsway Publications
Mr V. B. Lamb (Sussex Archaeological Society)

Miss K. G. Lee
Mr Peter Levi
The Librarian, University of Sussex
Miss Jean Mauldon
Mr Alan Neame
Mr F. J. Nicholson
The Oxford University Press
Messrs Pickering & Inglis
Psalms and Hymns Trust (Baptist Church House)
Mr Richards and Mrs Richards
Mrs Olive Russell
The Editor of 'The Scotsman'
The Rev. J. E. Seddon
The Society for Promoting Christian Knowledge
        (on behalf of the Registrars of Convocation of Canterbury
        and York)
Mrs D. E. Stranack
The Rev. E. C. D. Stanford
Miss M. G. Tulloch
Mr A. P. Watt
Miss Hella Young

Our list would be much longer if we included the names of all those who have given us advice and encouragement.

We have had some difficulty in tracing the sources of some of the versions. If we have omitted any acknowledgements to owners of copyright we apologise to them, and will rectify the omission in subsequent issues of this book.

K. H. STRANGE
R. G. E. SANDBACH